ADOBE® FRAMEMAKER® 9

CLASSROOM IN A BOOK®

The official training workbook from Adobe Systems

www.adobepress.com

Adobe

WHAT'S ON THE DISC

Here is an overview of the contents of the Classroom in a Book disc

Lesson files … and so much more

The *Adobe FrameMaker 9 Classroom in a Book* disc includes the lesson files that you'll need to complete the exercises in this book, as well as other content to help you learn more about Adobe FrameMaker 9 and use it with greater efficiency and ease. The diagram below represents the contents of the disc, which should help you locate the files you need.

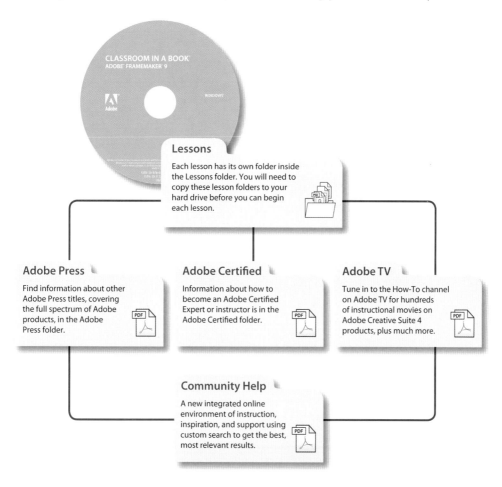

CLASSROOM IN A BOOK
ADOBE FRAMEMAKER 9

WINDOWS

Lessons

Each lesson has its own folder inside the Lessons folder. You will need to copy these lesson folders to your hard drive before you can begin each lesson.

Adobe Press

Find information about other Adobe Press titles, covering the full spectrum of Adobe products, in the Adobe Press folder.

Adobe Certified

Information about how to become an Adobe Certified Expert or instructor is in the Adobe Certified folder.

Adobe TV

Tune in to the How-To channel on Adobe TV for hundreds of instructional movies on Adobe Creative Suite 4 products, plus much more.

Community Help

A new integrated online environment of instruction, inspiration, and support using custom search to get the best, most relevant results.

CONTENTS

GETTING STARTED

Welcome to Adobe® FrameMaker® 9—a complete authoring and publishing solution for technical communicators. Its user-friendly interface, integrated workflows and toolsets, and a template-based authoring environment ensure efficient and consistent creation of your technical documents.

FrameMaker's redesigned interface is familiar to users of other Adobe applications. New floating toolbars and dockable dialog boxes let you customize your workspace for your own specific needs.

Book creation is now easier than ever with the new user interface and tools for creating hierarchical books. Incorporate XML files or reference DITA maps and other structured FrameMaker documents.

Whether you are creating complex multichapter documents with imported graphics, XML-based projects, or simple one-page memos, FrameMaker is the perfect solution, giving you power and flexibility.

FrameMaker offers a variety of export options including Adobe PDF (Portable Document Format), HTML, XML, print, and SGML, making it easy to repurpose and distribute complex content on multiple devices.

Edit your documents by importing PDF file comments from subject matter experts and other colleagues. The new user interface and Track Text Edits feature helps you manage your review processes.

FrameMaker offers a variety of other key features, including automated generation and updating of indexes, tables of contents, cross-references, and hyperlinks.

FrameMaker is part of Adobe's Technical Communication Suite, a major component of this powerful toolset for publishing technical content. For more information on the Technical Communications Suite, go to www.adobe.com/products/technicalcommunicationsuite.

About Classroom in a Book

Adobe FrameMaker 9 Classroom in a Book® is part of the official training series for Adobe graphics and publishing software developed by experts in association with Adobe Systems. These lessons are designed to let you learn at your own pace. If you're new to Adobe FrameMaker 9, you'll learn the fundamental concepts and features you'll need to master the program. If you've been using it for a while, you'll find this book teaches many advanced features, including tips and techniques for using the latest version of Adobe FrameMaker.

Although each lesson provides step-by-step instructions for creating a specific project, there is room for exploration and experimentation. It is recommended that you follow the book from start to finish, especially if you have never used FrameMaker before; but you can, if you wish, do only the lessons that correspond to your interests and needs. Platform or operating system differences are mentioned only when they are substantial.

Prerequisites

Before using *Adobe FrameMaker 9 Classroom in a Book*, you should have a working knowledge of your computer and its operating system. You should know how to use a mouse and standard menus and commands. You should also know how to copy, open, save, print, and close files. If you need to review these techniques, see your Microsoft® Windows or UNIX® documentation.

To review complete system requirements and recommendations for your Adobe FrameMaker 9 software, see the FrameMaker product page at www.adobe.com/products/framemaker.

Copying the Classroom in a Book files

The *Classroom in a Book* CD includes folders containing all the electronic files for the lessons. Each lesson has its own folder, and you must copy the folders to your hard drive to do the lessons. To save room on your drive, you can choose to install only the folder for each lesson as you need it, and remove it when you're done.

To install the *Classroom in a Book* files:

1 Make sure the *Adobe FrameMaker 9 Classroom in a Book* CD is in your CD-ROM drive.

2 Create a folder named FM_CIB on your hard drive.

3 Copy the lessons you want to the hard drive:

   • To copy all of the lessons, drag the Lessons folder from the CD into the FM_CIB folder.

   • To copy a single lesson, drag the individual lesson folder from the CD into the FM_CIB folder.

4 If you are installing the files in Windows, you need to unlock them before using them. You don't need to unlock the files if you are installing them in Mac OS.

Starting FrameMaker

When you start FrameMaker 9 for the first time, you are prompted to choose between two interfaces: the standard FrameMaker mode and Structured FrameMaker. This book is designed to work with standard FrameMaker mode.

To start Adobe FrameMaker in Windows

Do one of the following:

• Choose Start > Programs > Adobe > FrameMaker 9.

• Choose Start > Run, and then enter the full pathname of the program executable file, enclosed in double quotation marks (optionally followed by the name of a file to open): **"C:\Program Files\Adobe\FrameMaker 9\FrameMaker.exe"**.

To start Adobe FrameMaker in UNIX

In a UNIX window, do one of the following:

- To start the U.S. Edition, enter **maker**.

- To start the International Edition, enter **maker -l** (lowercase L) and the name of the language you want to use (for example, ukenglish, japanese, francais, or deutsch). For example, to start the French version of FrameMaker, you would enter **maker -l francais.**

Adobe FrameMaker 9 and Microsoft Word

Adobe FrameMaker 9 is especially compatible with Microsoft® Word and Microsoft Excel. This user-friendly capability makes it easy to import Word and Excel files into FrameMaker 9, and allows you to quickly utilize all its advanced authoring and document management tools.

Additional resources

Adobe FrameMaker 9 Classroom in a Book is not meant to replace documentation that comes with the program or to be a comprehensive reference for every feature in FrameMaker 9. Only the commands and options used in the lessons are explained in this book. For comprehensive information about program features, refer to any of these resources:

- **Adobe FrameMaker 9 Community Help**, which you can view by choosing Help > FrameMaker Help or by pressing F1. Community Help is an integrated online environment of instruction, inspiration, and support. It includes custom search of expert-selected, relevant content on and off Adobe.com. Community Help combines content from Adobe Help, Support, Design Center, Developer Connection, and Forums—along with great online community content so that users can easily find the best and most up-to-date resources. Access tutorials, technical support, online product help, videos, articles, tips and techniques, blogs, examples, and much more.

- **Adobe FrameMaker 9 Product Support Center**, where you can find and browse support and learning content on Adobe.com. Visit www.adobe.com/support/framemaker/.

- **Adobe TV**, where you will find programming on Adobe products, including a channel for professional photographers and a How To channel that contains hundreds of movies on FrameMaker 9 and other products across the Adobe Creative Suite 4 lineup. Visit http://tv.adobe.com/.

Also check out these useful links:

- The FrameMaker 9product home page
  (www.adobe.com/products/framemaker/).

- Resources for FrameMaker including user guides and tutorials
  (www.adobe.com/support/documentation/en/framemaker/).

- FrameMaker user forums (http://forums.adobe.com/community/framemaker)
  for peer-to-peer discussions.

- White papers and tutorials for Adobe FrameMaker
  (www.adobe.com/devnet/framemaker/tutorials_whitepapers.html).

- Read how companies and agencies are putting FrameMaker to use to
  enhance efficiency and productivity (www.adobe.com/products/framemaker/
  customerstories.html).

Adobe certification

The Adobe Certified Program is designed to help Adobe customers improve
and promote their product proficiency skills. The Adobe Certified Expert (ACE)
program is designed to recognize the high-level skills of expert users. Adobe
Authorized Training Centers (AATC) use only Adobe Certified Instructors to
teach Adobe software classes. The ACE program is the best way to master Adobe
products. For information on the Adobe Certified program, visit www.adobe.com/
support/certification/.

1 EXPLORING ADOBE FRAMEMAKER 9

Lesson overview

In this lesson, you'll learn how to do the following:

- Use the Welcome Screen

- Open a document with the Application Bar

- Work with tabbed documents

- Work with and dock panels and panel groups

- Display panels as icons

- Show and hide guides

- Use status bar controls

- Set up and manage a custom workspace

- Display rulers

 This lesson takes approximately one hour to complete. If you have not already copied the resource files for this lesson onto your hard drive from the Lesson01 folder on the *Adobe FrameMaker 9 Classroom in a Book* CD, do so now.

Getting started

FrameMaker 9 has an enhanced user interface that allows you to navigate and edit your documents with greater ease. Let's begin by examining this interface a bit.

First, of course, you'll have to launch FrameMaker. You can double-click its application icon or choose Start > Programs > Adobe > FrameMaker 9 > Adobe FrameMaker 9. (The specific path and names you see will vary depending on your OS and your installation of FrameMaker.)

When you open FrameMaker for the first time, you have the option of choosing Structured or Standard FrameMaker. If prompted, choose Standard FrameMaker. This book covers the creation of unstructured documents in FrameMaker 9. For more information on FrameMaker's structured capabilities, visit www.adobe.com/products/framemaker.

Using the Welcome Screen

Each time you launch FrameMaker, you will see the Welcome Screen. You will also see this screen whenever you don't have a document or book open in FrameMaker. This window gives you easy access to a variety of options, including:

*   Opening a recently viewed document

*   Creating a new FrameMaker document

*   Accessing FrameMaker templates

*   Accessing FrameMaker Help

The FrameMaker 9 Welcome Screen

To show you how easy it is, you will walk through one of those options here:

1   Click the New Features icon at the bottom left of the Welcome Screen.

    You are now viewing the FrameMaker 9 page on Adobe.com (provided you are connected to the Internet).

2 Click the Features link on the right side of the web page (under Product Info) to view a list of the new features in FrameMaker 9. When you are done exploring, close the browser window.

Opening a document

In this book, you will be working with documents that pertain to a fictional electronic device, called the Modul9. You will begin by opening one of those documents.

1 Still in the Welcome Screen, click the Open… icon to open an existing document.

2 Navigate to the Lesson01 folder on the *Adobe Framemaker 9 Classroom in a Book* CD.

3 Open the document entitled first_things_first.fm. For a breakdown of the FrameMaker workspace, see the screenshot below.

Text Formatting toolbar   Paragraph Formatting toolbar   Panels

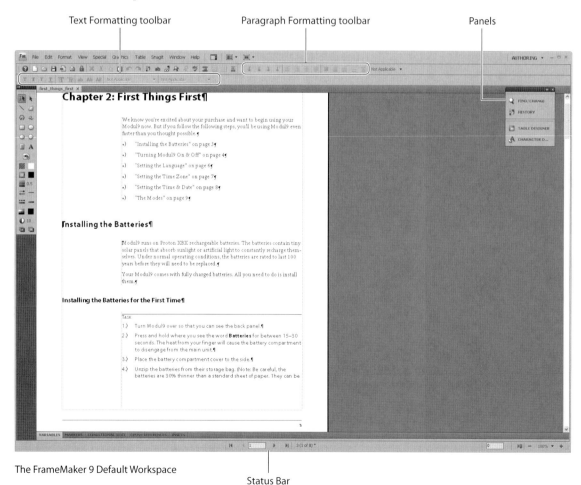

The FrameMaker 9 Default Workspace

Status Bar

4 Click on the File menu at the top of the screen and see the various commands listed there.

5 Scroll around on the page by using the scrollbars on the right sides of the FrameMaker window.

Next, you will begin working with the open document. Notice there are text symbols indicating line breaks, bulleted lists, and so forth. You will begin by turning them off for now.

6 Choose View > Text Symbols. Because this item was previously checked and you are choosing it, the text symbols toggle off. You will toggle them back on by doing the same process later.

Text symbols allow you to view non-printing characters like tabs and paragraph symbols in a document. Text symbols can be useful when editing FrameMaker documents, especially if they were created by another user.

FrameMaker's enhanced interface consists of an array of *panels, toolbars,* and *pods.* You can arrange them to your liking and save your custom grouping as a *workspace,* or select from preset workspaces. You can also hide much of the user interface with one click by selecting the UI Visibility button in the toolbar. You can turn text symbols back on (as shown below) by choosing View > Text Symbols.

The Quick Access Bar

The *Quick Access Bar*, located at the top of the FrameMaker window, contains application controls and menus. For example, you can open documents directly from the Application Bar.

Here, you will open another document from the FrameMaker CIB files folder, using the Quick Access Bar.

1 Click the Open icon, which resembles an open folder, on the Quick Access Bar.

2 Browse in the FrameMaker CIB folder for a document called cellphone.fm.

3 Select the filename, and click Open.

Working with tabbed documents

The *document window* shows the file you are currently working with, cellphone. fm. When you have multiple files open at once, they appear in a *tabbed view*, which allows you to easily switch from one document to another by clicking its tab.

Now you will choose the other open document, which will make it the active one.

1 Click on the tab for first_things_first.fm to bring that document to the foreground.

2 Click on the tab for cellphone.fm to bring that document to the foreground again.

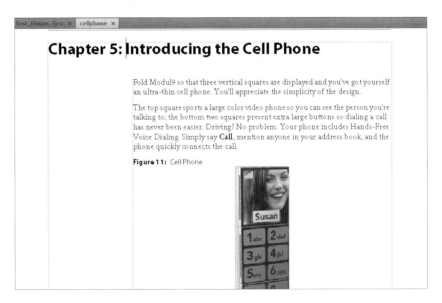

Next, you will explore the options to change the way your documents open in tabbed view. We will alter that option in the FrameMaker preferences.

Change the way open documents are displayed in the Interface Preferences dialog box.

Note: Preferences are settings that determine how FrameMaker will perform certain functions.

3   Choose File > Preferences > Interface. Deselect the Open Documents As Tabs option, and then click OK.

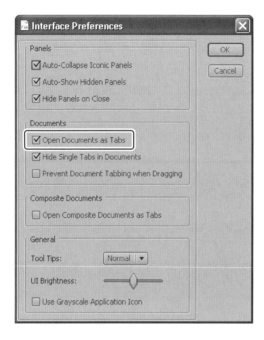

4   Choose File > Close to close all open documents, and choose No if prompted to save them.

5   Choose File > Open, and find and open first_things_first.fm. You will notice it does not open in tabbed view.

6   Press Ctrl+O to access the Open File dialog box, and choose cellphone.fm. Notice there are no tabs, although both files are now open.

Now, you will reset your Interface Preferences to allowing tabbed viewing.

7   Choose File > Preferences > Interface.

8   Select the Open Documents As Tabs option, and click OK.

When you are finished with this lesson and ready to move on to a new document, that document will now open in tabbed view.

Working with panels

Panels give you easy access to common features of FrameMaker, and can be arranged and customized to best suit your needs. Panels are located on the right side of the FrameMaker window, or can be accessed from the Window menu.

To see which panels are already opened in FrameMaker, and to open an unopened panel:

1 Choose Window > Panels. All panels that are open will be displayed with a checkmark in the list. If you don't currently have a document open, you'll need to do so before the Window > Panels option is active.

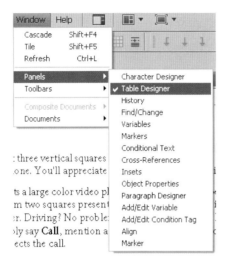

2 To open an additional panel, choose Window > Panels > Character Designer. This opens the Character Designer panel, which is used to format text. We will learn more about the Character Designer in a future lesson.

Panels displayed as icons

Panels can also be collapsed to icons in some cases, which can further reduce "clutter" in your workspace.

To demonstrate the icon view, you will collapse your panels to icon view, and click to display just the Character Designer panel.

To collapse all panels in a dock and display the Character Designer panel:

1   Click the double arrow at the top of the panel dock.

2   Resize the width of the dock until the text disappears by dragging the left edge toward the right.

3   Widen the dock until the text labels reappear.

4   Click once on the Character Designer icon or label to display its contents.

Docking panels

Panels can be docked and undocked to create custom configurations along the sides and bottom of the FrameMaker window. A *dock* is an arrangement of non-floating panels. Moving panels in and out of the dock is an easy process. You will test this by removing a panel from the doc and then redocking it.

1   To remove the Character Designer panel from its dock, drag it by its tab or title bar (the solid bar above the tab), and pull to the left of the screen. This figure shows that we clicked on the double arrow to collapse the panel to its icons.

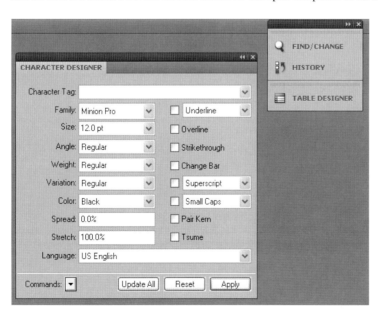

The Character Designer panel is now a *floating panel*—it is not connected to any other panels.

2 To redock the Character Designer panel, drag it by its tab into the dock. Look for the blue line between two panel groups that indicates you are dragging it to the dock, but not into another panel group. (You will see a blue line appear about the dock you are dragging it into.) You can place it at the top, bottom, or between other docked panels and panel groups.

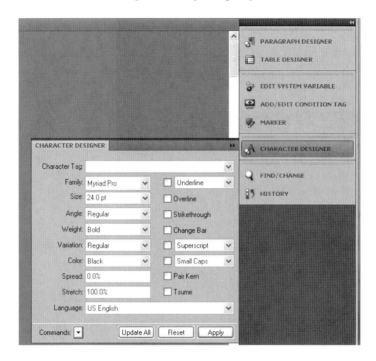

Using visual guides

You can show or hide several types of visual guides in a FrameMaker document, including borders around text and graphic frames, marker, symbols, and paragraph returns.

You will hide several of these, and then choose to show them again.

1 Be sure cellphone.fm is the active document.

2 Choose View > Borders.

The borders were showing previously, so choosing this hides the borders.

3 Choose View > Borders again to show the borders.

4 Choose View > Text Symbols to hide the text symbols.

5 Choose View > Text Symbols to show them again.

As you can see in the View menu, you can toggle off other visual cues as well.

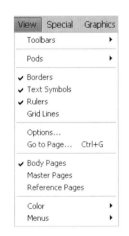

The status bar

The *status bar*, located at the bottom of the FrameMaker window, displays information about pagination and text formatting. It gives you easy access to navigation within your document, and zoom controls.

You'll get acquainted with some of the status bar functions by going to another page in the document, and then selecting another zoom view.

To go to another page in the document:

1 Click the right arrow located next to the current page field. This will advance you to the second page of the document.

Now you will change the zoom setting for the document.

2 Click the minus sign (-) to the left of the current zoom percentage, on the right side of the status bar. This will zoom the page to a smaller percentage.

3 Click the plus sign (+) to the left of the current zoom percentage, on the right side of the status bar. This will zoom the page to a larger percentage.

4 Click the arrow just to the right of the current zoom percentage, and choose a zoom setting from the menu. This menu allows you to choose from a predetermined set of zoom settings as well as to customize the zoom settings available in your document.

Rulers and units

You can specify the default increment for font size, line spacing, and other measurements for the document. Default units of measurement appear after the values in the text boxes. If you enter a value without a unit of measurement, FrameMaker uses the default unit.

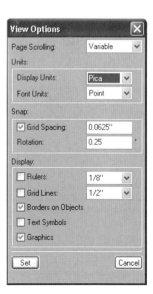

To change the unit of measurement for the current FrameMaker document:

1 Choose View > Options.

2 Click the arrow next to Display Units, and choose Pica from the list.

3 Click Set.

4 Choose View > Rulers to display the rulers for this FrameMaker document. Notice the rulers are now displayed in pica increments.

5 Choose File > Close to close this document.

Rulers are helpful when aligning objects or to set up guidelines for your FrameMaker document. You will explore these further in a future lesson.

Review questions

1 What is the Welcome Screen used for?

2 How do you zoom in on a document?

3 How do you display/hide text symbols?

4 How do you set your documents to display as tabbed documents?

Review answers

1 Use the Welcome Screen to access recently viewed documents, and to create new documents.

2 Click the plus sign (+) to the left of the current zoom percentage in the Status Bar.

3 Choose View > Text Symbols to show/hide the text symbols.

4 Go to File > Preferences > Interface. Select the box next to *Open Documents as Tabs*. Click OK.

2 FORMATTING DOCUMENTS

Lesson overview

In this lesson, you'll learn how to do the following:

- Explore templates
- Define paragraph formats
- Apply character formats
- Create a custom document
- Apply and delete formats
- Format heading and body text
- Format numbered and bulleted lists

 This lesson takes approximately 30 minutes to complete. If you have not already copied the resource files for this lesson onto your hard drive from the Lesson02 folder on the *Adobe FrameMaker 9 Classroom in a Book* CD, do so now. If needed, remove the previous lesson folder from your hard disk.

Chapter 4: Introducing Videoconferencing

When you flip to the Videoconferencing panel, you activate the latest in broadband videoconference technology. The Videoconferencing panel is a wireless videoconferencing unit that will allow you to set up and attend a videoconference over the Internet without a computer or other device. Because the Videoconferencing panel can send and receive video at up to 50 frames per second, you'll experience superior image and audio quality during each and every video-conference.

Figure 4: Videoconferencing Main Menu

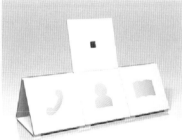

The main menu of the Videoconferencing panel consists of:

- A camera (at the top)
- The Call panel (at the left)
- The User Preferences panel (at the center)
- The Contacts panel (at the right)

About the Videoconference Camera

The camera is located at the top of the Videoconferencing panel. The camera automatically turns on the instant you begin a call, and turns off once the call is terminated.

Basic text features and formatting

A very logical place to start with FrameMaker is to begin using some of the text features of FrameMaker 9, and learn about formatting options.

Exploring templates

Begin by examining the list of templates that FrameMaker 9 provides to assist you in creating basic types of documents. New documents contain a basic set of predefined paragraph formats for headings, body text, numbered and bulleted lists, and other items.

1   Choose File > New > Document.

2   In the New dialog box, click the Explore Standard Templates button at the bottom-left corner.

3   Click Letter at the left side of the Standard Templates dialog box. The screen shows a sample letter-sized document.

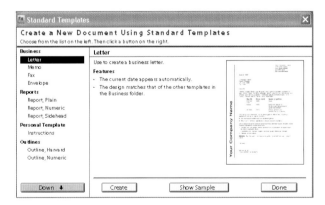

4 Click Memo.

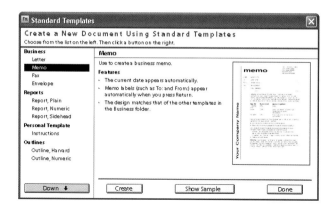

5 Click the Show Sample button. FrameMaker creates an untitled document with sample content for you to explore.

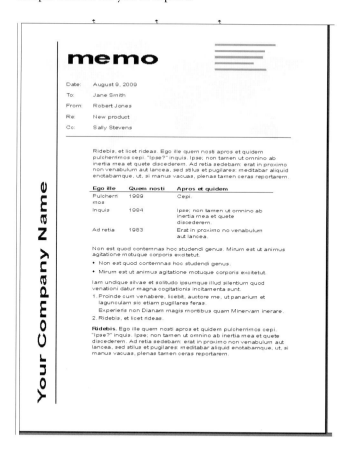

Here you will change the basic information on the memo to customize it.

6 Click to the right of the word To:, just under the date.

7 Type **Emma Jones** on the first line.

8 Press Enter.

9 Type **Modul9 Corporation** on the second line, after the word From:.

10 Press Enter.

11 Type **Modul9 Shipment Confirmation** on the third line, after the word Re:.

12 Choose File > Save As, and then type **Modul9_memo**, and then click Save.

13 Choose File > Close.

Customing your options

In the previous lesson, you were introduced to Modul9, a fictional electronic device used in the lessons through this book. In this lesson, you'll create a custom document and further explore the inferface and options of FrameMaker 9. You'll start by creating a custom document.

To see how your document will look at the end of this lesson, you can open videoconferencing_text.fm in the Lesson02 folder. When you're ready to continue, close videoconferencing.fm.

1 Choose File > New > Document.

2 Click Custom.

Click the arrow next to Inches to see the different units of increments FrameMaker offers. You have the option to change the default units for any document, so that measurements in dialog boxes will appear in the desired increment. For these exercises, you will use inches, but you will choose pica first, to see how FrameMaker can covert the measurements automatically for you.

3 Choose Pica from the Units menu, and notice all measurements in this window convert to picas.

4 Choose Inch from the Units menu.

5 In the Pagination area, select Double-Sided. Notice that in the Margins area, the text boxes formerly labeled Left and Right are now labeled Inside and Outside.

6 In the Page Size area, make sure the Width is 8.5 inches and the Height is 11 inches.

You can enter just the number (for example, 8.5 rather than 8.5 inches), because you have already specified inches as the units for the document.

7 Leave the Top and Bottom margins at 1 inch, but change the Inside and Outside margins to .75.

8 Click Create.

An untitled, blank document appears. If borders and text symbols are on, you see a dotted text frame border with an end-of-flow symbol (§) in the upper-left corner. This is the only text symbol you see, because the document doesn't contain any text yet.

9 If borders and text symbols are not visible, choose View > Borders and View > Text Symbols to see them.

10 Choose File > Save, make sure you are in the Lesson02 folder, enter the filename **Formats.fm**, and click Save.

Next, you'll turn on a typing aid that will help you work more efficiently.

11 Choose Format > Document > Text Options.

In the Text Options dialog box, Smart Quotes should already be selected. This tells FrameMaker 9 to insert the appropriate left or right curved quotation mark (" or ") when you type a quotation mark.

12 Select Smart Spaces, and click Apply.

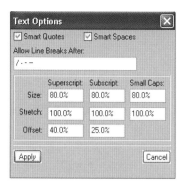

Smart Spaces prevents you from typing more than one standard (proportional) space in a row. This helps you keep spacing between words and sentences consistent. (Smart Spaces does not affect special fixed-width spaces, such as em spaces.)

Finally, you'll look at the paragraph formats stored in the document.

13 Click the Paragraph Formats arrow at the far-right side of the Paragraph Formatting toolbar. You will see a list of preformatted styles.

Later, you'll change these formats for your document.

14 Click the arrow at the top of the Paragraph Formats list to close the list.

Note: If the Unknown File Type menu appears, choose Microsoft Word, and click OK.

Copying text

It's easier to see whether text formats look the way you want when you have text in a document, so you'll import a text file into your blank document.

1 Choose File > Import > File.

2 Select videoconferencing_text.fm in the Lesson02 folder, and click Copy Into Document at the bottom of the dialog box. The text in this document already uses the paragraph tags that appear in the blank document. Click Import.

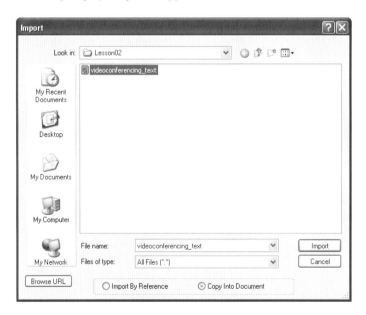

3 In the Import Text Flow By Reference dialog box, choose Retain Source's Formatting.

4 Click Import.

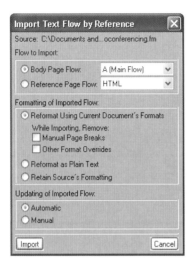

5 Click the First Page button in the status bar to display the first page of the document.

6 Click Ctrl+S. This is the keyboard shortcut to save a file.

Setting up rulers and the grid

Later in this lesson, you'll use the formatting bar and the top ruler to set indents and tabs for the text. You will continue to work in inches, but will also learn how to set some settings in picas and points. There are 6 picas in one inch and 12 points in one pica.

You'll also set up the invisible snap grid. Items in the top ruler (such as controls for tabs and indents) and objects on a page snap to this grid as you move them. This helps you place tabs, indents, and objects at regular intervals.

1 Choose View > Options.

2 Check to see that Inch is chosen in the Display Units menu.

<table>
</table>

Tip: Regardless of your current unit of measure, you can always enter a different unit by using the proper two-character abbreviation for that unit. For example:

- in indicates inches
- pt indicates points
- pc indicates picas

3 Enter **6 pt** (for 6 points) in the Grid Spacing text box in the Snap area of the View Options dialog box, and then click Set.

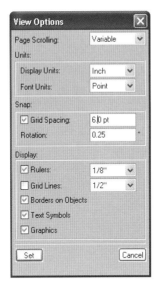

4 Click the Graphics menu once to open it. If a check mark appears next to the Snap command on that menu, it indicates that the Snap command is on. If there is no check mark or filled-in box, then the Snap command is not on.

5 If Snap is not on, choose Graphics > Snap. This will make it easier to select consistent numbers.

Creating a side-head area

Side heads are a great way to visually set headlines apart from body text. The side heads stand prominently to the side of the normal body text. You can set options for how the text lines up in conjunction with the body copy.

First baseline alignment

Major Mountains The Earth has two enormous mountain ranges. The Rocky Mountains and Andes run through North and South

Top edge aligment

Major Mountains The Earth has two enormous mountain ranges. The Rocky Mountains and Andes run through North and South

The formats you create for your Modul9 document will place second-level headings at the left edge of the text frame (indicated by the dotted border); other text will appear to the right of these headings. To achieve this effect, you'll set up a side-head area—an area on one side of the text frame that will contain headings.

1 Click anywhere in the first paragraph on page 1 to place an insertion point in the text.

2 Choose Format > Page Layout > Column Layout.

3 Select Room For Side Heads.

4 In the Room For Side Heads area, change Width to **1.275** and Gap to **.194**.

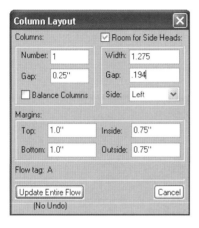

5 Click Update Entire Flow.

6 Click OK in the dialog box telling you all type will reflow, and cannot be undone.

All the text moves into the right side of the text frame. The side-head area appears to the left, but it's empty. In the next exercise, you'll change the format of the headings so that they extend across or move into the side-head area.

Formatting headings

To redefine the formats for two levels of headings, you'll use the Paragraph Designer. The Paragraph Designer creates and changes paragraph formats in your document quickly and easily.

About the Paragraph Designer

Note: You can choose to set the Paragraph Designer as a floating panel by dragging its top bar to separate it from the dock. Drag it to a position that doesn't obstruct your document, and keep the panel open until you've made all of your changes.

Before you start formatting the actual headings, take a moment to become familiar with the Paragraph Designer and its properties, starting with displaying it.

1   Choose Format > Paragraphs > Designer.

   The Paragraph Designer appears.

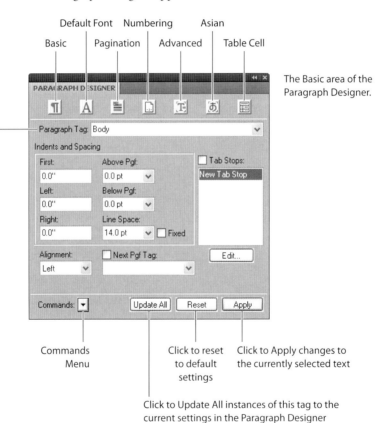

Default Font   Numbering   Asian

Basic   Pagination   Advanced   Table Cell

The Basic area of the Paragraph Designer.

Current Paragraph Tag

Commands
Menu

Click to reset
to default
settings

Click to Apply changes to
the currently selected text

Click to Update All instances of this tag to the
current settings in the Paragraph Designer

At the top of the Paragraph Designer panel are icons for displaying the different categories of paragraph properties, such as Basic, Default Font, and Pagination.

Below the icons is the Paragraph Tag menu, showing the style assigned to the currently selected paragraph.

Below the Paragraph Tag menu are controls for the currently selected tab (Basic) including indents and spacing and the Tab Stops section.

At the bottom of the Paragraph Designer panel is the Commands menu, useful for creating a new format and deciding how to apply a certain format throughout your document.

2   Click the Default Font icon ¶ at the top of the Paragraph Designer. The Default Font properties appear below the list of icons.

3   If you like, display any of the other groups of properties.

Redefining formats with the Paragraph Designer

Now you'll use the Paragraph Designer to redefine the paragraph formats for two levels of headings.

Formatting first-level headings

First you'll make first-level headings span the side-head area and the body-text area. In this document, these headings are all tagged Heading1.

1 Click anywhere in the heading *Introducing Videoconferencing.*

2 In the Paragraph Designer, click the Pagination icon at the top of the panel.

3 On the right side of the Paragraph Designer, click Next Pgf in the Keep With area. This forces the heading to stay on the same page as the first lines of the paragraph that follows the heading.

4 In the Format area, select Across All Columns And Side Heads. This allows first-level headings to span both areas of the text frame.

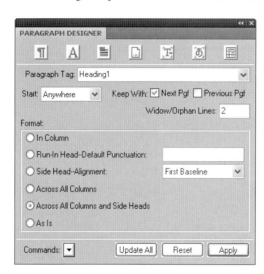

The Pagination area of the Paragraph Designer.

5 At the bottom of the Paragraph Designer, click Update All. (If FrameMaker 9 notifies you that some paragraphs use format overrides, click Remove Overrides.) This changes all paragraphs tagged Heading1 and also changes the Heading1 format in the Paragraph Catalog.

The heading moves to the left edge of the text frame.

Next, you'll change the font properties of Heading1 paragraphs.

6 In the Paragraph Designer, click the Default Font icon (¶) at the top of the panel.

7 Change the Size to **20**. Make sure the Weight is Regular. The value 20 does not appear in the menu, so you must enter it in the Size text box.

8 Click Update All.

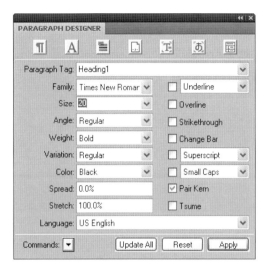

Finally, you'll change the paragraph and line spacing to reduce the space between the heading and the body text that follows it.

9 Click the Basic Icon (¶) at the top of the Paragraph Designer..

10 Change the Below Pgf to **0** and the Line Space to **20**, and then click Update All.

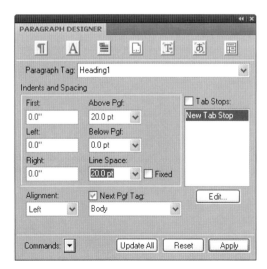

Formatting second-level headings

The second-level headings in the document are all tagged Heading2.

1 Navigate to page 3.

2 Click in the heading *Focusing*. Note that this paragraph is already formatted with a style of Heading 2.

3 In the Paragraph Designer, display the Pagination properties.

4 In the Format area, select Side Head with Alignment setting of First Baseline, and click Update All. (If FrameMaker 9 notifies you that some paragraphs use format overrides, click Remove Overrides.)

Any Heading2 paragraphs in your document move into the side-head area.

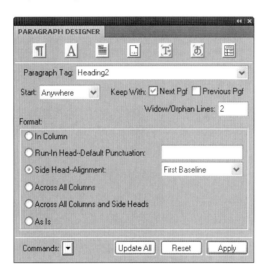

5 Display the Default Font properties.

6 Change the Family to Myriad Pro, the Size to 10, and the weight to Bold. Click Update All.

Finally, you'll add some space between the Heading2 paragraphs and the preceding body text.

7 Display the Basic properties.

8 In the Indents And Spacing area, change Above Pgf to 20 and Below Pgf to 0, and click Update All.

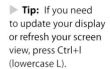 **Tip:** If you need to update your display or refresh your screen view, press Ctrl+l (lowercase L).

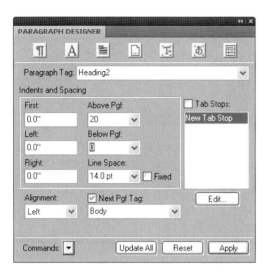

Formatting text elements

Beyond the obvious "body text," many documents may share a significant number of other common text elements, such as bulleted and numbered lists and tabbed or columnar data. In this section, you'll format many of these elements.

Body text

The ordinary paragraphs in the current document are tagged Body. You'll change the font, make the type size smaller, and add space between the lines.

1 Click in a paragraph of body text on page 3.

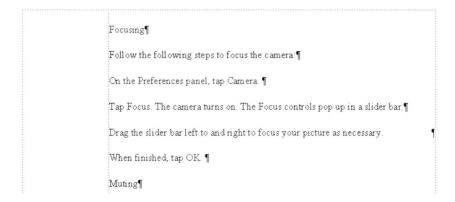

2 In the Paragraph Designer, display the Default Font properties.

⬤ **Note:** Spread
(sometimes called
tracking) adds or
subtracts space
between characters for
a looser or tighter look.

3 Change the Family to Myriad Pro (Windows) or Myriad, the Size to 9, and the Spread to 5.

4 Click Update All. (If FrameMaker 9 notifies you that some paragraphs use format overrides, click Remove Overrides.)

Next, you'll change the paragraph and line spacing.

5 Display the Basic properties.

6 In the Indents And Spacing area, change Above Pgf to **5**, the Line Space to **13**, and then click Update All.

Finally, you'll indent the first line of the paragraph. The indent symbols appear in the top ruler. Notice the triangles, one on top of the other. The top triangle symbolizes the first-line indent, and the second triangle symbolizes the remainder of the paragraph.

⬤ **Note:** In a paragraph
format, indents and
tabs are measured from
the edge of the text
frame margin, not the
edge of the page.

7 Drag the first-line indent symbol to the right, to the next ruler marking. Because you turned on Snap earlier in this lesson, the indent symbol snaps to the next ruler marking.

The First setting in the Paragraph Designer changes to .156".

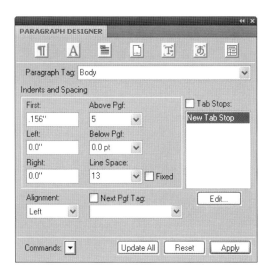

Notice that the indent changed only in the paragraph that contains the insertion point. You need to assign the change to all the Body paragraphs.

Note: Clicking the double arrow at the top right of the Paragraph Designer collapses it to an icon. To expand it, click the double arrow again.

8 In the Paragraph Designer, click Update All. The first ine of all Body paragraphs are now indented.

Numbered lists

Numbered lists are a way of displaying sequential information. This is helpful in many instances, for example, when indicating steps to perform in a specific order.

You'll learn to create two paragraph formats for numbered lists: one for the first item in a list, and the other for subsequent items in the list. The first will number the paragraph (or item) with a 1; the second will increment each item by 1.

All numbered steps will use a hanging indent—that is, the number will appear at the left margin, and the text will be indented from the left margin.

Creating a format for the first item in a list

Rather than modify an existing format, you'll create a new format. The items you want to number are already formatted as body paragraphs.

1 Click in the Page Status field in the status bar, and type **7**. Page 7 is now displayed.

2 Below the heading *Option Description*, click in the paragraph that begins with *DCS 2.0.*

3 In the bottom-left corner of the Paragraph Designer, click the Commands arrow and choose New Format from the menu.

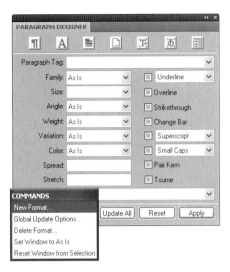

4 Enter **Step1** in the Tag text box.

5 Make sure that the options Store In Catalog and Apply To Selection are selected, and click Create.

The tag of the current paragraph changes to Step1, and the Step1 format is added to the Paragraph Catalog.

Next you'll use the rulers and formatting bar to set up indents and a tab stop.

6 In the ruler, drag the first-line indent symbol back as far to the left as it will go.

7 Drag the left indent symbol to the next ruler marking to the right.

You'll use a tab stop to set the space between the item number and the text that follows it.

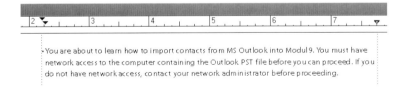

Left-aligned (and other) tab stops

In FrameMaker, tabs can be left-aligned, center-aligned, right-aligned, or decimal-aligned. The tab well area in the formatting bar contains icons for applying any of these alignments. You'll want a left-aligned tab stop for the current listing.

Simply drag a left-aligned tab stop from the tab well to just under the left indent. Notice that the settings for the tab stop appear in the Paragraph Designer.

In the Paragraph Designer, click Update All. The appearance of the paragraph doesn't change, because you haven't yet added a tab character. You'll do that when you set up automatic numbering.

Setting up numbering for the first item

A document can use automatic numbering for different types of items (for example, numbered steps, numbered chapters, and sections). An autonumber format may include a series label that specifies an independently numbered series and building blocks that serve as placeholders for numbers or letters. An autonumber format may also include tabs, text, and punctuation.

You'll finish the Step1 paragraph format definition by setting up its autonumber format.

1   In the Paragraph Designer, display the Numbering properties.

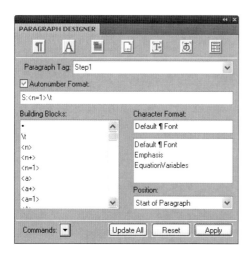

2   Type **S:** (the uppercase letter S followed by a colon) in the Autonumber Format text box. This is the series label you'll use for items in a numbered list—in other words, the title you give to that set of formatting, which you will apply to other items within the document.

3 Select <n=1> in the Building Blocks scroll list. This building block, which will insert the number 1 in the paragraph, appears in the text box.

4 Select \t in the scroll list to add a tab character to the autonumber format.

5 Click Update All. The autonumber appears at the beginning of the paragraph. The tab character is represented by the tab symbol.

6 Choose File > Save.

Formatting subsequent numbered items

Now you'll create a paragraph format for the subsequent numbered items in a list. (This format will increase the step number of each successive item by 1.) You'll begin by applying the Step1 format to the other paragraphs in the numbered list, because that format is very close to the format you want. Then you'll create a new paragraph format for the paragraphs, and change the autonumber format.

1 Drag to select the three paragraphs below the numbered step.

2 Choose Step1 from the Paragraph Formats menu in the formatting bar. This menu contains all the formats in the Paragraph Catalog. You can apply formats from this menu just as you apply them from the catalog.

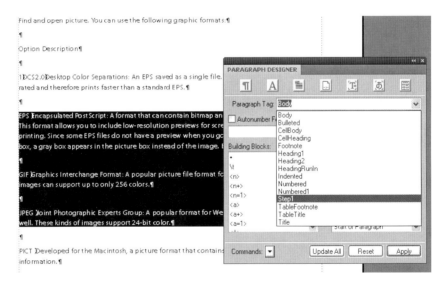

All the selected paragraphs now begin with the number 1, but you'll fix that next.

3 In the Paragraph Designer, choose New Format from the Commands menu.

4 Enter **Step** in the Tag text box.

5 Make sure that the options Store In Catalog and Apply To Selection are selected, and click Create.

6 Delete everything after the colon in the Autonumber Format text box.

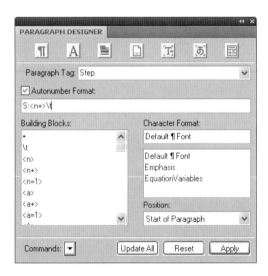

7 Select <n+> in the Building Blocks scroll list. This building block will increment by 1 the number of the previous paragraph in the series.

8 Select \t in the Building Blocks scroll list to add a tab character, and then click Update All.

9 Click anywhere in the document to deselect the text.

10 To see how the document looks without the text symbols, choose View > Text Symbols.

You are about to learn how to import contacts from MS Outlook into Modul 9. You must have network access to the computer containing the Outlook PST file before you can proceed. If you do not have network access, contact your network administrator before proceeding.

Formatting bulleted lists

Next, you'll create a format for items in a bulleted list. You'll work with the Step1 format as a base, because it's very close to the format you want.

1 Go to page 9 of the document by clicking the Page Status area in the status bar, typing **9** in the Go To Page dialog box, and clicking Go.

2 Select the paragraph next to the heading *Import Contacts*.

3 Choose Step1 from the Paragraph Formats menu in the formatting bar.

   All the selected paragraphs are numbered 1.

4 In the Paragraph Designer, choose New Format from the Commands menu.

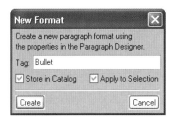

5 Enter **Bullet** in the Tag text box.

6 Make sure the options Store In Catalog and Apply To Selection are selected, and then click Create.

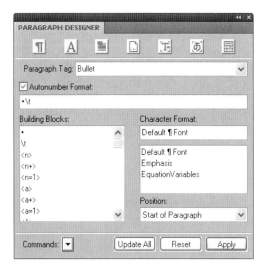

7 Delete the contents of the Autonumber Format text box.

8 In the Building Blocks scroll list, select \b.

   This building block inserts a round bullet symbol at the beginning of each Bullet paragraph.

9 Select \t in the Building Blocks scroll list to insert a tab, and then click Update All.

10 Click anywhere on the page to deselect the paragraphs.

Next, you'll change the left indent of the bulleted paragraphs.

11 Click in the first bulleted paragraph.

12 In the ruler, drag the left indent symbol as far to the left as it will go (to the left margin).

The paragraph no longer uses a hanging indent.

13 In the Paragraph Designer, click Update All to update the other bulleted items and the Bullet format in the catalog.

14 If you like, apply the Bullet paragraph format to the items under the next heading.

Formatting a chapter title

All that's missing now is the chapter title. You'll add the title and create a new chapter title format.

1 Go to page 1.

2 Choose View > Text Symbols.

3 Click at the beginning of the first paragraph on the page, and press Enter to create an empty paragraph.

4 Click in the empty paragraph, and type **Modul9 Video** (the text of the title).

The paragraph format for the chapter title will be similar to the Heading1 format, so you'll start with that format.

5 In the formatting bar, choose Heading1 from the Paragraph Formats menu.

6 In the Paragraph Designer, choose New Format from the Commands menu.

7 Enter **ChapterTitle** in the Tag text box.

8 Make sure the options Store In Catalog and Apply To Selection are selected, and then click Create.

9 Display the Default Font properties in the Paragraph Designer.

10 Change the Size to **30**. This value does not appear in the menu, so you must enter it in the Size text box.

11 Change the Font to Myriad Pro and the weight to Bold, and then click Update All.

12 Display the Basic properties in the Paragraph Designer.

● **Note:** Paragraph tags must be all one word, no spaces.

Tip: You can feed in the building block either by typing it or selecting it from the scroll list.

13 Change Below Pgf to **18**, and click Update All.

14 Display the Numbering properties.

15 Populate the Autonumber Format text box with **C:Chapter**x **<n+>**. (Be sure to enter a space before the <n+> building block.)

This autonumber format tells FrameMaker to number chapters in a different sequence than steps (the series label is C: rather than S:) and to begin the paragraph with the word Chapter followed by a space and the chapter number.

16 Add a colon and a space at the end of the text in the Autonumber Format text box, and click Update All.

When you assemble the chapters into a book, they will be numbered sequentially.

17 Close the Paragraph Designer.

Deleting formats

When you created the document, its Paragraph Catalog already contained some paragraph formats that you won't use. You'll delete the unused formats.

1 Click the Paragraph Catalog arrow on the upper-right side of the document window to display the Paragraph Catalog.

2 At the bottom of the catalog, click the Commands arrow, and choose Delete Format.

3 Select Bulleted (not Bullet) in the scroll list, and then click Delete Format.

4 Select HeadingRunIn, and Click Delete Format again.

5 Delete the Indented, Numbered, Numbered1, and Title (not ChapterTitle) formats.

6 Click Done. Notice that the formats you deleted no longer appear in the Paragraph Catalog.

7 Close the Paragraph Catalog.

8 Save and close the document.

For in-depth information about formatting text, visit www.adobe.com/support/framemaker.

Review questions

1   How do you create a new custom document?

2   What is the effect of turning on the invisible snap grid?

3   List three options for positioning headings and other paragraphs in a document that has a side-head area.

4   How do you change the definition of a paragraph format?

5   How do you create a new paragraph format?

6   What items can you include in an autonumber format?

Review answers

1   Choose File > New > Document (Windows) or choose New from the main FrameMaker 9 window (UNIX). Click Custom, set the options for the document, and click Create.

2   With the grid turned on, items in the ruler and objects in the document snap to the invisible grid when you move them. This helps you position tab stops, indents, and objects at regular intervals.

3   The paragraphs may appear in the side-head area, in the body-text area, or across all columns and side heads.

4   In the Paragraph Designer, you change properties of the format, and then click Update All.

5   In the Paragraph Designer, choose New Format from the Commands menu. Enter a tag for the format, specify whether the format is stored in the catalog and applied to the selection, and click Create.

6   An autonumber format may include a series label, a building block for an automatically inserted number or a bullet, a building block for a tab, and text.

3 PAGE LAYOUT

Lesson overview

In this lesson, you'll learn how to do the following:

- Change the column layout

- Display master pages

- Create and position page headers and footers

- Number pages using system variables

- Create running headers and footers

- Create custom master pages

 This lesson takes approximately one hour to complete. If you have not already copied the resource files for this lesson onto your hard drive from the Lesson03 folder on the *Adobe FrameMaker 9 Classroom in a Book* CD, do so now. If needed, remove the previous lesson folder from your hard disk.

Chapter 4: Introducing Videoconferencing¶

When you flip to the Videoconferencing panel, you activate the latest in broadband videoconference technology. The Videoconferencing panel is a wireless videoconferencing unit that will allow you to set up and attend a videoconference over the Internet without a computer or other device. Because the Videoconferencing panel can send and receive video at up to 50 frames per second, you'll experience superior image and audio quality during each and every videoconference.¶

Figure 4: Videoconferencing Main Menu¶

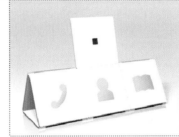

The main menu of the Videoconferencing panel consists of:¶

•)   A camera (at the top)¶

•)   The Call panel (at the left)¶

•)   The User Preferences panel (at the center)¶

•)   The Contacts panel (at the right)¶

About the Videoconference Camera¶

The camera is located at the top of the Videoconferencing panel. The camera automatically turns on the instant you begin a call, and turns off once the call is terminated.¶

Getting started

Page layouts for FrameMaker 9 documents are stored on special master pages—one master page for each layout used in a document. The master pages define column layouts for text and the contents and placement of headers and footers. The master pages also may contain background text or graphics that appear on the corresponding body pages.

To learn how page design works in FrameMaker 9, you'll set up the page layout for the chapters of a small book. You'll learn how and where to work with the column layout and the master pages. The sample document already contains the paragraph and character formats that you'll use for document text.

Changing column layout

You'll begin by narrowing the page margins so more text will fit on each page.

1   Open videoconferencing.fm in the Lesson03 folder.

2   Choose File > Save As, enter the filename **videoconferencing1.fm**, and click Save.

3   Make sure the document is set to use inches as the unit of measurement (if necessary, choose View > Options, select Inches as the Display Units increment, and then click Set).

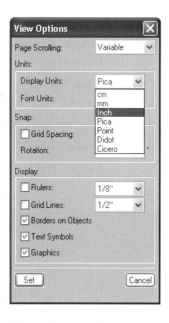

4   Choose Format > Page Layout > Column Layout.

5 In the Margins area, set the Bottom to **.875** and leave the Inside and Outside margins at .75.

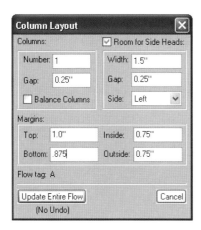

6 Click Update Entire Flow. The pages will now reflect the changes you have made.

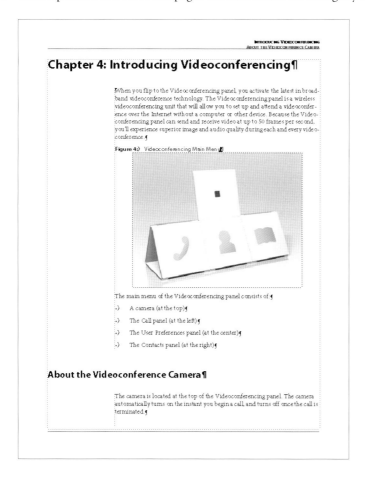

Displaying master pages

A document's *master pages* contain the layouts for the *body pages* that contain the document's contents. Every FrameMaker 9 document has at least one master page. The videoconferencing1.fm document has two master pages, because it's a double-sided document; one master page is used for all the left pages, and another is used for all the right pages.

1   Choose View > Master Pages to display the master page that determines the layout of the current body page.

The name of the master page (Left or Right) appears in the page status area of the status bar. The page status area also tells you whether this is the first or second of the two master pages.

2   Click in the large text frame on the Right master page. This is a body text frame (also referred to as a *template text frame*), which provides the layout for the text frames in which you type on body pages.

Flow: A ¶: Body

The tag area in the status bar shows you the *flow tag*—the name of the text flow that the text frame belongs to.

Most documents contain one main text flow that runs from the first page to the last. By default, this flow is tagged as *A*. When text extends beyond a body page, FrameMaker 9 adds a new page automatically, using the same master page as was currently being used, and continues the text on the new page.

3   Click in the header text frame at the top of the page. This text frame and the footer text frame at the bottom of the page are used for the headers and footers that appear on body pages. Everything included in these frames will show up on all subsequent pages in the document.

¶: ~Header

Header and footer status bars don't contain flow tags, and FrameMaker considers them background text frames.

As you'll see, the contents of background text frames appear on body pages, but they are *background text*—text that can be edited only on the master pages.

▷ **Tip:** If your text frame is selected (you will see the eight selection handles), you can double-click the box to place the cursor in the box.

4   On the Right master page, click in the footer area, and type **Modul9**. If the name appears as a gray bar instead of readable text, click the Increase Zoom button in the status bar until the text is big enough to read.

Modul9|

5 Choose View > Body Pages to display the body pages. Go to the first page of the document, using the status bar.

Modul9 appears at the bottom of the page, but the background text frame's borders are not displayed. If you click on the text that you added to the footer, you'll see that you can't get an insertion point, because the text isn't editable on the body page.

6 Click the Next Page button in the status bar to display page 2.

Modul9 doesn't appear at the bottom of page 2, because this is a left-hand page—it uses the Left master page, whose background text frames are still empty.

7 Click the Next Page button again.

Modul9 does appear on page 3, because it's a right-hand page and, like page 1, it gets its page design from the Right master page.

8 Choose View > Master Pages and display the Left master page.

9 Click in the footer on the Left master page.

10 Type **Modul9**.

Modul9

11 Choose View > Body Pages, and click in the status bar to view any left page. Notice that the text has automatically updated.

Headers and footers

As previously stated, master pages define structure for multipage documents. Headers and footers are an important part of that structure; they can supply any number of consistent, repeating (or subsequent) elements in a document, such as chapter and section titles, page numbers, and any other reference points you might want to include.

Numbering pages

You make page numbers appear on the pages of your document by inserting a page number *system variable* on the master pages. System variables are placeholders for system information such as the page number, page count, date, and filename.

You'll add the page number at the top of every page. The paragraphs in the header and footer text frames are tagged Header and Footer.

You'll set up page numbering so that the numbers appear on the right side of right-hand pages and on the left side of left-hand pages. You're on the Right master page now, so you'll use the left-aligned tab stop to left-align the page numbers.

1   Navigate to the Right Master page.

2   Click in header.

3   Position your cursor in the header, at the far-left edge.

● **Note:** You can also insert this variable from the Special > Variables panel.

4   Choose Format > Headers & Footers > Insert Page #.

A number sign (#) appears at the left side of the header text frame. It will be replaced by the page number on the body pages.

Next, you'll insert the page number variable in the header of the Left master page.

5   Click the Previous Page button in the status bar to display the Left master page. The name of the master page appears in the Page Status area of the status bar.

6   Click in the header text frame and press Tab to move your cursor to the right side of the header.

7   Choose Format > Headers & Footers > Insert Page #. The number sign appears at the right margin. This is where you want page numbers to appear on left-hand pages.

Footer formats typically aren't stored in the Paragraph Catalog, because you usually don't need to apply these formats to paragraphs on the body pages.

The asterisk in the status bar indicates that the Header paragraph format doesn't match a format in the catalog. The paragraph format for the paragraph in the header text frame contains center-aligned and right-aligned tab stops (shown in the top ruler). Even though the Header paragraph style is not in the Paragraph Catalog, you can still use the Paragraph Designer to control it.

You will change the font used in the Header paragraph. Since the Header paragraph format is used on the Left and Right master pages, you can update both header paragraphs at the same time.

8   Be sure you are on the Right master page, and click in the header text frame.

9 Choose Format > Paragraphs > Designer to display the Paragraph Designer.

10 Click the Default Font icon at the top the Paragraph Designer.

11 If necessary, choose Myriad Pro from the Family pop-up menu and Bold from the Weight pop-up menu, and click Update All. Remove Overrides, if prompted.

12 Close the Paragraph Designer.

13 Choose View > Body Pages to display the body pages again. The page number now appears on each page. If you want, scroll through the document to see how the page number alternates between the left and right sides.

14 Save the document.

Creating running headers and footers

If you want the same text to appear in the footer of every page, you can simply type the text in the background text frames on the master pages. But you can also create a header or footer using a variable. For this document you'll use a Running Header/Footer variable—a master-page element whose text depends on the contents of the page.

For example, a running footer (or header) based on Heading1 paragraphs contains the text of the first Heading1 paragraph on the page. If the page doesn't contain a Heading1 paragraph, the footer uses the text of the most recent Heading1 paragraph on preceding pages.

Like a page number, a running header or footer is created by inserting a system variable on a master page rather than by typing text. The running footers for this document will contain the chapter title and a first-level heading.

1   Choose View > Master Pages to display a master page. If you're not already there, navigate to the Right master page.

2   Click in the footer text frame and delete the text you entered earlier (Modul9). (You may need to scroll down to see this text frame.)

The footer will appear on the right side of right-hand pages and on the left side of left-hand pages. You're on the Right master page, so you'll use a tab stop to right-align the footer.

3   Press Tab. The insertion point moves to the right margin of the footer text frame.

Next, you'll replace the phrase Modul9 with a variable that displays the chapter title. Select and delete the text Modul9.

4   Choose Format > Headers & Footers > Insert Other.

5   Scroll down in the Variables list until you see Running H/F 1. This is one of 12 system variables provided specifically for running headers and footers.

6 Single-click the Running H/F 1 variable and note the definition of the variable appears in the scroll list.

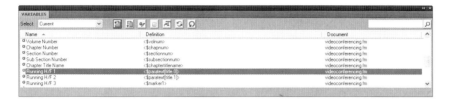

The definition uses the paratext *building block*, which tells FrameMaker 9 to use the text of a paragraph with the tag that follows in square brackets. The definition specifies the Title paragraph format. Your chapter title uses the title.0 format, which is already set up for you. Double-click the Running H/F 1 variable to insert it into your footer. Note: you could have easily selected the variable from the Variables pod without going to the Format menu item.

Running H/F 1|

Finishing the footers

To finish the footers, you'll change their paragraph format and then copy the formatted footer variables to the other master page.

1 Choose Format > Paragraphs > Designer to display the Paragraph Designer.

2 Click the Default Font icon at the top of the Paragraph Designer, change the Family to Myriad Pro, the Size to 8 (points), the Weight to Bold, and the Spread to 10.

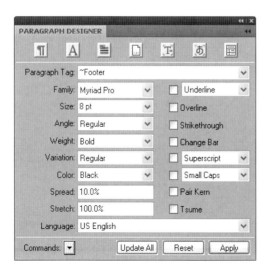

Note: You can access the Paragraph Designer in a variety of ways:

- Choose Window > Panels > Paragraph Designer
- Choose Format > Paragraphs > Designer
- Use the Keyboard Shortcut, Ctrl+M

3 Click Update All, allow Format Overrides if prompted, and close the Paragraph Designer.

Running H/F 1|

Now you'll insert the footer variable in the footer of the left master page.

4 Navigate to the Left master page and place your cursor in the footer.

5 Remove the existing Modul9 text, and insert a Running Header/Footer 1 variable from the Variables pod.

Running H/F 1|

6 Choose View > Body Pages to display the body pages again, and scroll through the document. The running footer now appears on each page.

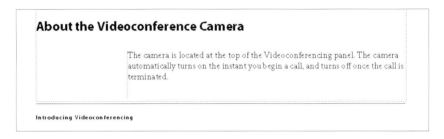

7 Save the document.

● **Note:** FrameMaker 9 allows you to define and use as many as 12 different running headers and footers in a document. This can be very useful if you want different headers and footers on different page layouts, such as the first page of a document.

Custom master pages

In addition to typical left and right master pages, you can (within reason) create as many custom master pages as your documents might require. For instance, many types of documents use custom master pages for different types of content.

In this exercise, you will create an entirely new master page, and learn how to customize it.

Note: Although a FrameMaker document can contain more than 100 different master pages, most often you'll use only a few.

Creating a custom master page

First you will create a master page based on an existing one, and one from scratch.

1   Go to page 1 of videoconferencing1.fm, and click anywhere inside the text frame.

2   Choose View > Master Pages to display the master page currently applied to page 1.

3   Choose Special > Add Master Page, and enter **Start** in the Name text box.

4   Choose Right from the Copy From Master Page menu in the Initial Page Layout area, and then click Add. If prompted to continue, click OK.

Now you'll create a second custom master page that won't be based on the Right or Left master page.

5   Choose Special > Add Master Page, and enter **Last** in the Name text box.

6   Select Empty in the Initial Page Layout area, and then click Add.

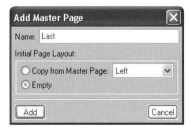

7   Save the document.

Modifying a custom master page

You can define different headers and footers, change margins, and change the column layout in custom master pages.

1 Go to the newly created Start master page.

2 Choose View > Toolbars > Graphics Toolbar to display the Tools palette.

3 Select the Select Object cursor ( ) from the top-right corner of the Tools palette. (You will work with other tools in the Tools palette in Lesson 5.)

4 Click anywhere in the header of the Start master page to select this background text frame.

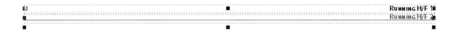

There may be situations where headers and footers are not needed on certain pages.

5 Delete the header text frame by pressing Delete.

6 Delete the footer in the same way.

Start (3 of 4) *

Now you'll customize a master page by creating a main body page frame and second text frame in which you can type your own notes separately from the rest of the document text flow.

7 Go to the master page called Last.

8 Select the Place A Text Frame tool () from the Tools palette to add a new text frame.

9 Draw a moderate size box, as shown here.

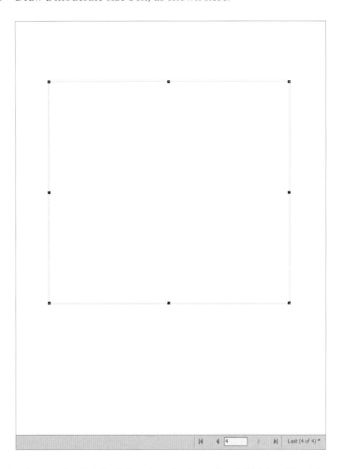

10 After you've finished drawing the box, the Add New Text Frame dialog box appears. If it does not, you've likely inserted a Graphics Frame. Delete and create a frame using the Text Frame tool. Select the Template For Body Page Text Frame option in the Text Frame Type area, and notice "A" is selected in the Flow Tag box. Click Add.

11 Draw a smaller text box near the bottom of the Last master page, as shown here.

12 When the Add New Text Frame dialog box appears, type **B** for the Flow Tag, and then click Add.

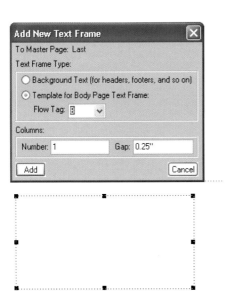

13 Select the Select Object tool from the upper-right corner of the Tools palette, and click on the larger text frame. Choose Graphics > Object Properties.

14 Change the Width to **6** and the Height to **4**. In the Offset From area, change the Top offset to **1** and the Left offset to **1.25**. Make sure the Tag is set to A. Make sure Autoconnect and Room For Side Heads are both selected, and then click Set.

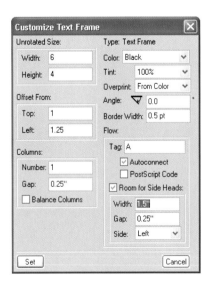

15 With the Select Object tool still selected in the Tools palette, click on the smaller text frame.

16 Choose Graphics > Object Properties.

17 Change the Width to **3.5** and change the Height to **2**. In the Offset From area, change the Top offset to **8** and the Left offset to **2.5**.

18 Make sure the Tag is set to **B**, deselect Room For Side Heads, and click Set.

For in-depth information about variables, page layout, and templates, visit www. adobe.com/support/framemaker.

Note: FrameMaker offers you an alternate way to apply certain master pages to a page or group of pages, via Format > Page Layout > Master Page Usage. Choose from a dropdown menu of currently available Master Pages, and apply individually or to a string of pages.

Review questions

1 How do you change the page margins of a document?

2 What are master pages?

3 What are the main differences between the template for body page text frames and the background text frames that appear on master pages?

4 How do you insert a page number in a header or footer?

Review answers

1 To change page margins, choose Format > Page Layout > Column Layout, specify new margins, and click Update Entire Flow.

2 Master pages are pages that contain layouts for body pages. Master pages also contain header and footer information, and they may contain background text or graphics that appear on the corresponding body pages.

3 The template for body page text frames provides a layout for the text frames on body pages. The template for body page text frames has flow tags and is copied to body pages. Background text frames, such as those for headers and footers, have no flow tags and are not copied to body pages. The contents of background text frames appear on body pages, but the contents can be edited only on master pages.

4 To insert a page number, go to a master page, click in a header or footer text frame, and insert a Current Page # variable by double-clicking. You can also choose Format > Headers & Footers > Insert Page #. The actual page numbers will appear on the body pages that use that master page.

4 DEFINING COLORS AND CHARACTER FORMATS

Lesson overview

In this lesson, you'll learn how to do the following:

- Define custom colors and tints
- Use color in paragraph formats
- Create character formats
- Use a character format in paragraph autonumbers
- Apply a character format to words and phrases

 This lesson takes approximately 30 minutes to complete. If you have not already copied the resource files for this lesson onto your hard drive from the Lesson04 folder on the *Adobe FrameMaker 9 Classroom in a Book* CD, do so now. If needed, remove the previous lesson folder from your hard disk.

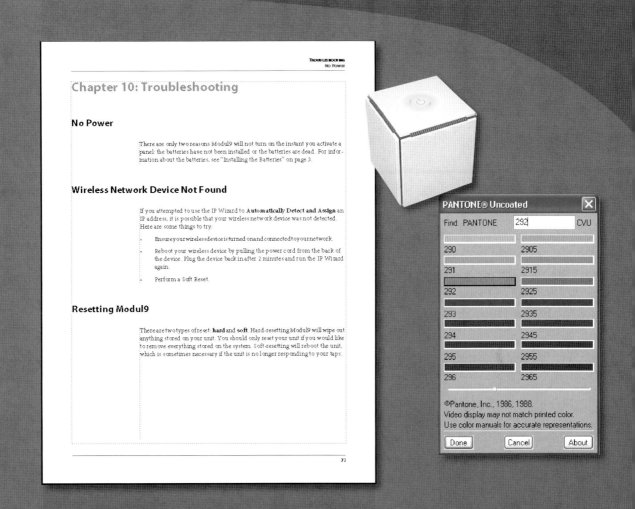

Chapter 10: Troubleshooting

No Power

There are only two reasons Modul9 will not turn on the instant you activate a panel: the batteries have not been installed or the batteries are dead. For information about the batteries, see "Installing the Batteries" on page 3.

Wireless Network Device Not Found

If you attempted to use the IP Wizard to **Automatically Detect and Assign** an IP address, it is possible that your wireless network device was not detected. Here are some things to try:

- Ensure your wireless device is turned on and connected to your network.
- Reboot your wireless device by pulling the power cord from the back of the device. Plug the device back in after 2 minutes and run the IP Wizard again.
- Perform a Soft Reset.

Resetting Modul9

There are two types of reset: **hard** and **soft**. Hard-resetting Modul9 will wipe out anything stored on your unit. You should only reset your unit if you would like to remove everything stored on the system. Soft-resetting will reboot the unit, which is sometimes necessary if the unit is no longer responding to your taps.

PANTONE® Uncoated

Find: PANTONE 292 CVU

290	2905
291	2915
292	2925
293	2935
294	2945
295	2955
296	2965

©Pantone, Inc., 1986, 1988.
Video display may not match printed color.
Use color manuals for accurate representations.

[Done] [Cancel] [About]

Getting started

All FrameMaker 9 documents include some basic color definitions, and the standard templates also provide character formats for changing the appearance of words and phrases. When you're setting up templates or creating custom documents, you can define other colors and create your own character formats.

In this lesson, you'll define a color to use for headings, autonumbers, and for selected words and phrases.

You can define a color by specifying exact color values. In this case, however, you'll use a predefined color from one of the color libraries that come with FrameMaker 9. These libraries contain colors that can be matched precisely by commercial printers.

Defining custom colors and tints

Color is an effective way to draw the eye to text and objects you want to emphasize. Every FrameMaker 9 document includes definitions for several standard colors.

1 Open troubleshooting.fm in the Lesson04 folder.

2 Choose File > Save As, enter the filename **troubleshooting1.fm**, and click Save.

3 Choose View > Color > Definitions.

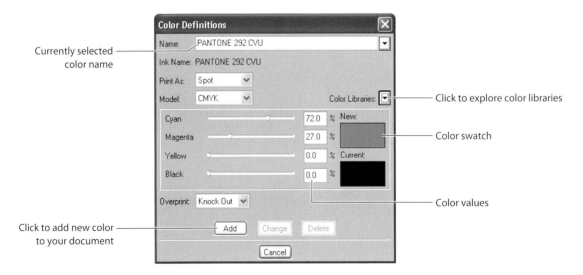

4 Choose PANTONE® Uncoated from the Color Libraries menu.

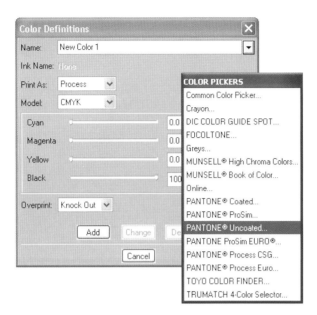

5 At the top of the PANTONE Uncoated dialog box, enter **292** in the Find text box.

The list in the dialog box scrolls to show you the PANTONE color you specified.

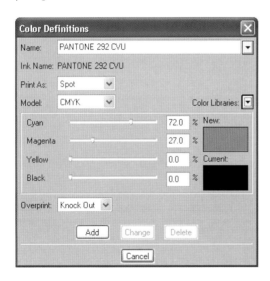

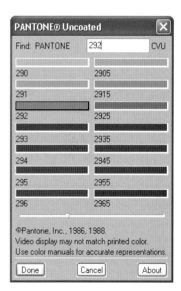

6 Click Done to select the color.

7 Click Add to include the new color in your document.

8 Click Done to exit and close the Color Definitions dialog box.

FrameMaker 9 displays a swatch of the color in the New area and inserts the corresponding color values—percentages of cyan, magenta, yellow, and black—in the dialog box. These four colors can combine to represent most of the visible colors.

Adding color to paragraph formats

The subheads in the troubleshooting document are currently black. You'll change their paragraph formats so they appear in the Pantone color you just added.

1 Click in the chapter title in the Paragraph Designer (if the Paragraph Designer panel is not visible, choose Window > Panels > Paragraph Designer to display it).

2 From the icons at the top of the Paragraph Designer, choose Default Font.

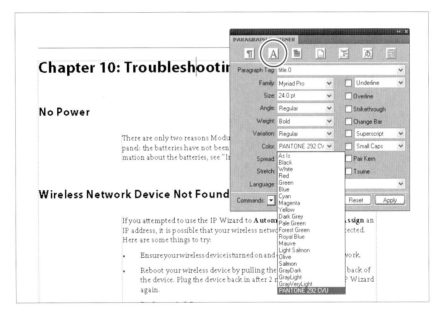

3 Choose Pantone 292 CVU from the Color menu, and click Update All. The chapter title appears in color.

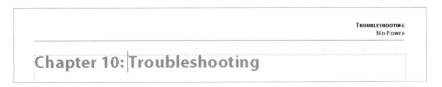

4 Save the document.

Adding color to autonumbers

In numbered lists, the automatically inserted numbers currently appear in black, but you'll make them appear in color. You will do this by adding a *character format*. Character formats are used for characters, words, or phrases rather than for whole paragraphs. A character format can change one or more text properties.

Creating a character format

To add color to the bolded text, you'll create a character format.

1 Go to page 1, and select the bolded text in the second paragraph.

2 Choose Window > Panels > Character Designer to display the Character Designer. The Character Designer works in the same way as the Paragraph Designer, but it contains only the Default Font group of properties.

Notice the character format (Character Tag) is called high.bold.

3 Choose Pantone 292 CVU from the Color menu.

4 Click the Commands arrow at the bottom left of the Character Designer and choose New Format.

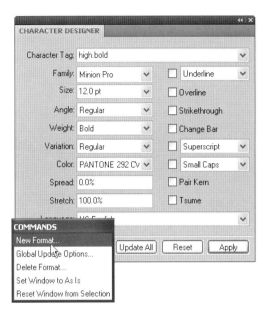

5 Name the new style **highblue.bold**, verify that both Store in Catalog and Apply to Selection are selected, and click Create.

The bolded text is now colored with the Pantone color.

If you attempted to use the IP Wizard to Automatically Detect and Assign an IP address, it is possible that your wireless network device was not detected. Here are some things to try:

Applying the character format for autonumbers

Now that you've defined the character format, you can use it to add color to automatically inserted numbers. Your document uses two paragraph formats for numbered paragraphs (one for the first, and the other for the rest of them), so you'll apply the character format you create to the numbering options for both paragraph formats.

1   Navigate to page 2, and click the insertion point in the first numbered paragraph on page 2, under the heading "Perform a Hard Reset."

2   In the Paragraph Designer, notice the style is step.begin in the Paragraph Tag menu.

3   Click the numbering icon at the top of the Paragraph Designer and choose highblue.bold from the list on the right side. Click Update All.

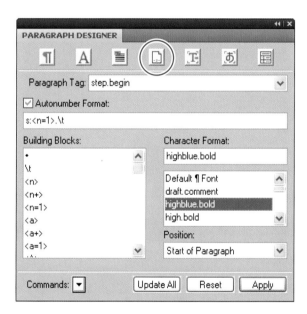

The autonumber of the first numbered paragraph now appears in color. You'll make the same change to the paragraph format for the other numbered paragraphs.

TASK

1.   Turn Modul9 over.

4   Click in the second numbered item. Notice the Paragraph Tag is step.continue.

5   Click the numbering icon at the top of the Paragraph Designer and choose highblue.bold from the list on the right side. Click Update All. If you are prompted, Remove All Overrides. All the numbers now appear in color.

6   Save the file.

For in-depth information on working with color in FrameMaker, see Adobe Help.

Review questions

1 What kinds of color definitions can you use for a document?

2 How can you make all paragraphs with a particular format (such as subheads) appear in color?

3 How do you display the Character Designer? How do you display the Character Catalog?

Review answers

1 All FrameMaker 9 documents include some basic color definitions. You can add custom color definitions by specifying color values or by choosing the colors from a library.

2 Add color to the paragraph format. To do this, display the Default Font properties of the Paragraph Designer, choose a color from the Color menu, and click Update All.

3 To display the Character Designer, choose Format > Characters > Designer or Control-D. To display the Character Catalog, choose Format > Characters > Catalog.

5 WORKING WITH GRAPHICS

Lesson overview

In this lesson, you'll learn how to do the following:

- Adjust frames for graphics
- Import a graphic
- Mask part of an imported graphic
- Draw lines and rectangles
- Change drawing and graphic properties
- Move, resize, align, distribute, and group graphic objects
- Use the History panel

This lesson takes approximately one hour to complete. If you have not already copied the resource files for this lesson onto your hard drive from the Lesson05 folder on the *Adobe FrameMaker 9 Classroom in a Book* CD, do so now. If needed, remove the previous lesson folder from your hard disk.

Chapter 5: Overview of the GPS Panel

You'll never get lost again thanks to your Modul9 GPS system.

The GPS panel allows you to view your current geographic location anywhere in the world and is accurate within two feet. Once your location has been determined, you can plot a course from your current location to nearly any address or location in the world. You can create hot spots that mark any location. Once a hot spot has been defined, you can create **routes** and **tracks** on graphic maps stored with Modul9's memory module. You can then plot a course between any two hot spots.

Figure 12: GPS Panel

Using the GPS panel is simple. Flip Modul9 to the GPS panel. You will see six squares. Four squares will display a map; the other two squares contain the GPS menu and navigation cues. When the GPS panel is activated, Modul9 instantly begins communicating with dozens of GPS satellites circling the globe. Once Modul9 has established a connection with at least two satellites, your current location will appear on a map at the left and a menu will appear at the right.

Press the **Guide Me** button on the button, select a Hot Spot from your Hot Spot list (or search for a destination by address, city, state, road name or type of attraction) and within seconds you will see and hear audible turn-by-turn directions, an estimated time of arrival at your destination and more.

Customizing master pages

In FrameMaker, you can draw or import graphics to add visual interest to a page design or to illustrate your document. You can also specify graphic properties such as fill pattern, pen pattern, line width, and color, and you can resize, reshape, rotate, and rearrange graphics.

In this lesson, you'll add master page graphics to complete the page design of the sample chapter you've been working on. You'll import one graphic and draw others. When you're finished, the graphics you add to the master pages will appear on each body page. (This is the purpose of master pages—to provide a consistent "background layer" for as many repetitive elements as you might want your document pages to have.)

1   To start this lesson, open cellphone_GPS.fm in the Lesson05 folder.

2   Choose File > Save As, enter the filename **cellphone_GPS1.fm**, and click Save.

Adjusting header and footer frames for graphics

Before adding graphics to headers and footers, you'll reposition the header and footer frames on each master page. (As was briefly mentioned earlier, the function of master pages is to provide consistent "backdrop" content that will automatically show up on as many document pages as you specify.)

The document is set to 100% zoom. Don't change it for now.

If the header and footer text appear as gray bars rather than as text, don't worry. The text is just *greeked*—that is, it's represented by a substitute for real text at this magnification. You'll zoom in later.

Changing the Right master page

The header and footer text frames on the master pages were created automatically by FrameMaker 9 when the document was created. You'll reposition the header and footer on the Right master page, which is one of the default pages created by FrameMaker for a Facing Pages document.

First you'll move the page header closer to the right edge of the page. You'll use the rulers at the top and left sides of the document window to help you position the header text frame. Note that the ruler markings are in inches.

1 Choose View > Rulers. The rulers appear at the top and left side of the document.

2 Choose View > Master Pages. FrameMaker 9 displays the master page controlling the Body page containing the cursor. In this case, the Right master page is displayed.

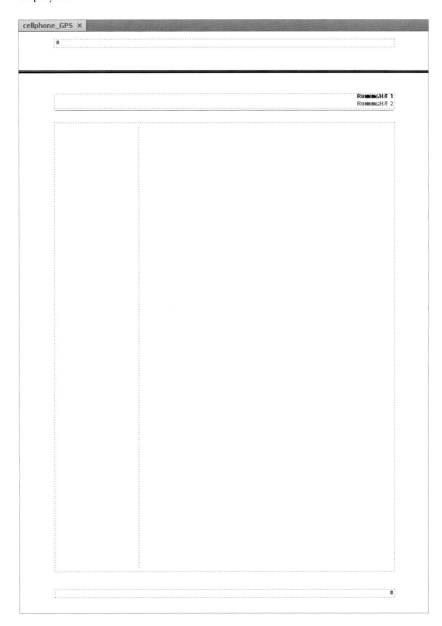

Before you reposition objects, you'll make sure that the snap grid is on. (Objects snap to the grid as you drag or resize them.)

3 Click the Graphics menu and choose Snap, if it is not already turned on. A check mark or filled-in check box next to the Snap menu item indicates the Snap command is on.

Note: You can also select the Select Object tool in the Tools palette, but this is a handy shortcut.

Note: Holding down Shift as you drag constrains the movement to only horizontal or only vertical.

4 Select the header text frame by Ctrl-clicking it. Handles appear around the header text frame.

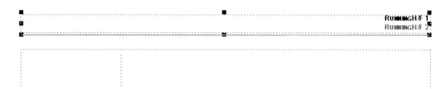

5 Place the pointer inside the header text frame (not on a handle). The pointer changes to a hollow arrow.

6 Shift-drag the header text frame to the right until the right edge of the text frame is at the 8-inch mark on the top ruler.

Vertical lines appear below the ruler as you drag, to indicate the left side, center, and right side of the frame.

The header text frame still needs to move a little more to the right, so you'll adjust its position slightly.

7 To move the header text frame four points to the right, press Alt+Right Arrow four times (using the arrow key to the left of the numeric keypad).

Next, you'll move the header text frame closer to the top of the page.

8 To move the header text frame four points to the right, press Alt+Right Arrow four times (using the arrow key to the left of the numeric keypad).

9 Next, select the line that was below the text frame and press delete.
Next, you'll move the header text frame closer to the top of the page.

10 With the header text frame still selected, Shift-drag upward until the y axis is set to .375. You can find the y axis at the bottom-left corner of the status bar.

Changing the Left master page

Now you'll reposition the header and footer text frames on the Left master page to make the left and right pages symmetrical.

1 Click the Previous Page button in the status bar to display the Left master page.

2 Ctrl-click the header text frame to select it.

3 Shift-drag the header text frame to the left until the left edge of the frame is at the ½ inch mark on the top ruler.
Next, you'll move the header text frame closer to the top of the page.

4 With the header text frame still selected, Shift-drag it upward until the y axis is set to .375. You can find the y axis at the bottom-left of your the bar.

5 Save the document.

● **Note:** The actual distance moved depends on the current zoom setting, so that you can do finer work when you're zoomed in closer. For example, at 200% magnification, the keyboard shortcut nudges .5 point. At 100% magnification, the object would move 1 point; at 50%, 2 points.

● **Note:** The x axis is the horizontal positioning of the selected item from the left edge of the document; the y axis is the vertical positioning of the selected item from the top edge of the document.

Working with graphics

In this section, you'll import graphics (and learn the two methods of doing so), get acquainted with some of the tools in the Graphics Toolbar, work with various graphic-altering techniques, and draw basic shapes.

Importing a graphic

When you are importing graphics, you have two options:

- Import By Reference
- Copy Into Document

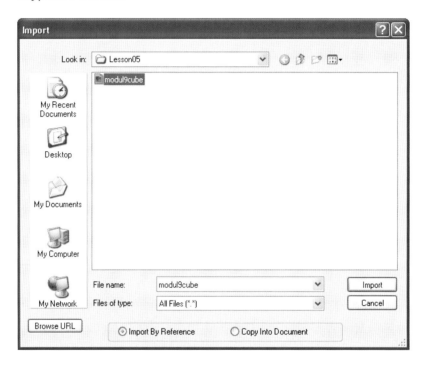

When you use Copy Into Document, a copy of the original graphic is stored in the document. There are two advantages to this method:

- If you move the document—for example, bring it to a print shop—the graphics are already contained in the document.
- You don't have to depend on the original graphic file. The original graphic can be changed, moved to a different directory, or deleted without affecting the copies in your document.

However, if the graphic requires adjustments and the original graphic file is updated, it will not update in the FrameMaker document. It will need to be re-imported to reflect the changes.

When you use Import By Reference, the graphic file isn't stored in the document. Instead, the document contains a pointer to the original graphic file. There are two advantages to this method:

- The file size does not increase by the file size of the image; instead, it contains only a pointer to the stored graphic file on the disk. This can greatly reduce the size of a file. (If you import by using Copy Into Document on both the Left and Right master pages, the document contains the same image twice, increasing the file size.)

- The graphic in the document will be updated automatically whenever the stored graphics file is changed. (If you import by copying and then change the graphic file, you need to reimport the graphic to update the image stored in the document.)

The page design used with this document calls for a graphic to appear at the top of each page. The graphic was created in another application and saved as a TIFF. You'll import the graphic and position it on the page.

In this exercise, you'll import the graphic by reference.

1 If necessary, scroll up until you see the top of the Left master page.

2 Click in the page margin to make sure that nothing is selected on the page and that there's no insertion point.

3 Choose File > Import > File.

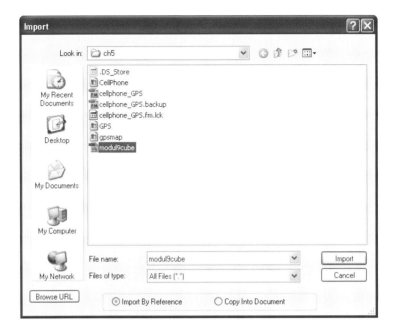

4 Open the folder called "Lesson05."

5 Select Import By Reference, and then select modul9cube.tif from the list.

6 Click Import.

The Imported Graphic Scaling dialog box appears.

7 Select 72 dpi (dots per inch) to set the scaling for the graphic, and click Set.

▶ **Tip:** If you plan to print your document, a good standard resolution is 300 dpi (dots per inch), and for online viewing only, choose 72 dpi.

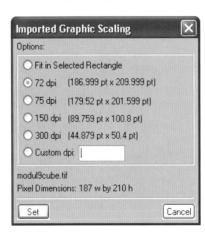

The graphic is centered on the page.

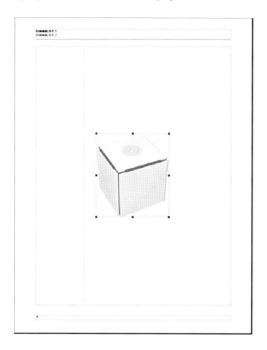

Note: If the graphic is cropped by a text frame, appears in an anchored frame, or doesn't appear at all, you probably had an insertion point when you chose File > Import > File. Choose Edit > Undo, click outside the text frames, and try again.

Next, you'll reposition the graphic to the top of the page.

8   With the graphic still selected, choose Graphics > Object Properties.

9   In the Offset From area, change the Top offset to **8pt**, change the Left offset to **6pt**, and then click Apply. The graphic moves up to just below the header, and resizes to fit into place above the body text frame.

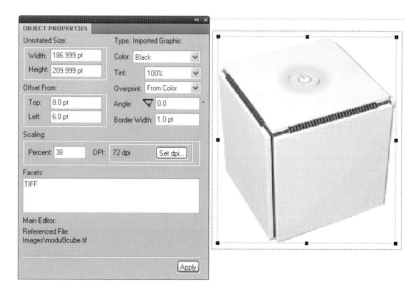

10 Use the Runaround Properties panel to set the Style to Run Around Bounding Box.

11 Repeat the process on the Right master page, and move the graphic to line up with the right edge of the Header.

12 Save the document.

Masking part of a graphic

Next, you will learn how to mask part of a graphic. Masking involves cropping a graphic so only part of it shows. It is important to know the rest of the graphic is still there but is hidden. You will hide the top portion of the cellphone.

1 Go to the first page of the document.

2 Click on the outside dotted line of the graphic to select the graphic frame.

3 Position your cursor at the top center handle until the downward arrow appears.

4 Drag down until the arrow reaches the top of the keypad.

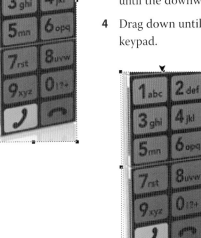

The top portion is hidden, and can easily be redisplayed if you change your mind, by dragging the handle up again.

5 Save your document.

Copying and altering graphics

You'll alter the graphic on the Left master page and copy it to the Right master page. You'll also flip the graphic for a symmetrical look.

1 Choose View > Master Pages.

2 On the Left master page, click the Modul9cube graphic to select it.

3 Hold down Shift, and drag a corner handle to resize the graphic a bit. Notice that the entire group resizes at the same time.

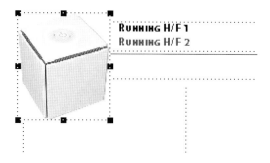

4 Still holding down Shift, drag the graphic to the right of the page, and up a bit, so the graphic sits at the y axis of .44".

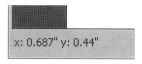

Notice the rule runs over the graphic box. You'll fix this next.

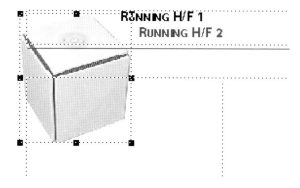

5 Right-click on the graphic, and choose Send To Back.

6 Choose Edit > Copy.

7 Navigate to the Right master page, and choose Edit > Paste. The graphic appears at the top of the page, in the same position as on the Left master page.

Now, you will flip the graphic horizontally.

8 Right-click again, and choose Flip > Left/Right.

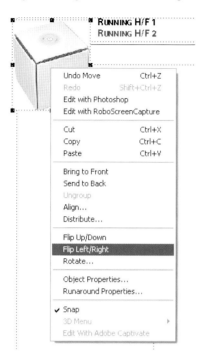

9 With the graphic still selected, choose Graphics > Send To Back. The header text frame reappears.

10 If you want, choose View > Body Pages to display the first page of the document, and then scroll through the document to see the modified headers and footers. When you're finished, choose View > Master Pages, and make sure the Right master page is displayed.

11 Save the document.

Drawing lines

The next step in this page design involves creating a line (also called a *rule*) that will appear at the bottom of each page.

Because the snap grid is on and is set to .625" (you can check this under View > Options), when you draw an object, it will "jump" in size in 5/8" increments.

For finer control, you'll turn off the Snap command now.

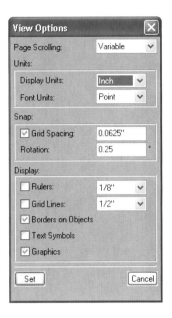

1 Choose Graphics > Snap to turn off the snap grid.

2 If necessary, navigate to the Right master page, and scroll down until you can see the footer.

3 Select the Draw A Line tool () in the Tools palette.

4 Choose Solid from the Pen pop-up menu.

5 Choose the second line width from the Line Width pop-up menu.

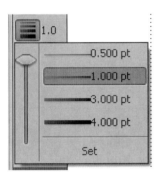

The default value for the second line width is 1.0 point.

6 In the Tools palette, make sure that the line end is set to No Arrow, the line style is set to Solid, the color is set to Black, and the tint is set to 100%.

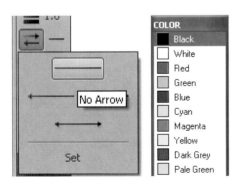

● **Note:** If the line is thicker than one point, choose Set on the Line Width pop-up menu, click Get Defaults, and choose the second line width from the Line Width pop-up menu again.

7 Move the pointer to the document window. The pointer changes to a crosshair (+).

8 Shift-drag from just above the left side of the page footer to draw a horizontal line that extends to the right edge of the page. (Don't drag beyond the edge of the page.)

The line appears a few points above the text frame.

9 If you want to adjust the vertical position of the line, do one of the following to move the line one point at a time:

- (Windows) Press Alt+Up Arrow or Alt+Down Arrow (using the arrow keys to the left of the numeric keypad).

- (UNIX) Press Ctrl+Up Arrow or Ctrl+Down Arrow.

A brief digression into History

There are times when you might want to see your last action. The History panel allows you to do just that—see the steps you just completed.

Choose Window > Panels > History. (If there is a checkmark next to History, the panel is already showing, and you don't need to choose it.) Notice that your last few actions are displayed in the History panel in the order in which they were performed. This can be helpful to see if you already completed a certain step, or want to see where you left off, or need to revert back to a previous document state.

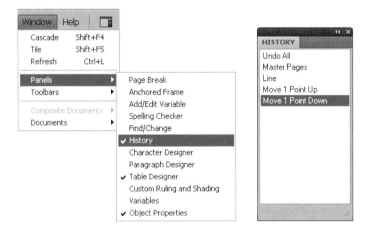

Drawing one more rectangle

To finish the footer, you will add a rectangle to the master page.

Now you'll draw the rectangle.

1   Select the rectangle tool (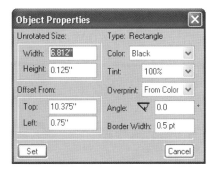)in the Tools palette.

2   Choose Solid from the Fill pop-up menu.

3   In the document window, drag to draw a rectangle below the left edge of the horizontal line and end it just to the left of the page number. The rectangle should be approximately 6.812" wide and .125" high (the dimensions appear in the status bar as you drag). Don't worry about the exact placement of the rectangle—you'll fix that next.

Tip: You can set drawing properties before you draw an object, or you can select the object after it is drawn and change its properties (choose Object Properties from the Graphics menu). Whatever property you select remains the current property until you change it.

4   Close the Tools palette.

Positioning objects

FrameMaker gives you options for aligning your objects, and for distributing space between multiple objects. You will learn about these features next.

Aligning objects

You have the graphics you need (the line and the rectangle), and the line is in the position you want. Now you need to place the rectangle correctly in relation to the line. FrameMaker 9 provides two commands, Align and Distribute, that change the positions of objects with respect to each other. You'll use these commands now.

1   With the small rectangle you created in the previous section still selected, Shift-click the horizontal line to add it to the selection.

2 Choose Graphics > Align. The Align panel opens.

You'll align the left sides of the rectangle and the line.

3 In the Top/Bottom area, select As Is to leave the vertical alignment unchanged.

4 In the Left/Right area, select Left Sides, and click Align.

Distributing objects

The left side of the rectangle is aligned with the left endpoint of the line. (The last object selected—the line—doesn't move. Other selected objects—in this case, the rectangle—move until the objects are aligned with the last-selected object.)

1 Make sure the rectangle and line are both selected, and then choose Graphics > Distribute.

2 In the Horizontal Spacing area, select As Is, so that you don't change the horizontal spacing.

3 In the Vertical Spacing area, select Edge Gap, and make sure the edge gap is set to 0.

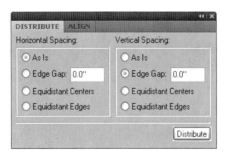

4 Click Distribute. The rectangle moves up until it touches the line—that is, the gap between them is 0.

5 Choose Graphics > Group to group the two objects.

A single set of handles now appears around the grouped set of objects.

6 Save the document.

To complete the page design, you'll copy the line and rectangle to the Left master page.

7 With the grouped objects still selected, right-click, and choose Copy.

8 Click the Previous Page button in the status bar to display the Left master page. As before, don't click anywhere on the page. (If you click inside a text frame, the graphic will be pasted inside the frame instead of at the bottom of the page.)

9 Choose Edit > Paste. The graphic appears at the bottom of the page, in the same position as on the Right master page.

The page design is finished.

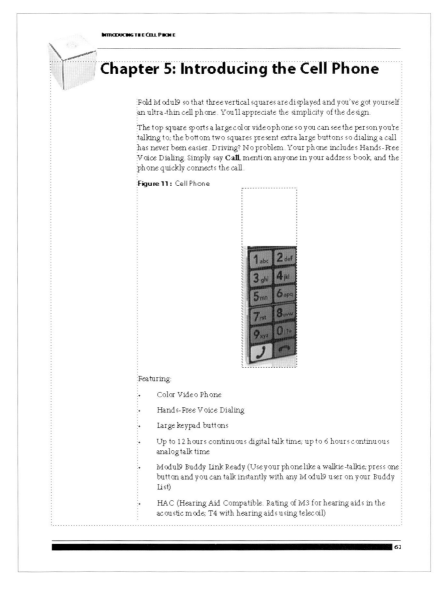

10 Choose View > Body Pages to display the first page of the document, and then scroll through the document to see the modified page design.

11 Save and close cellphone_GPS1.fm.

For in-depth information about graphics, visit www.abobe.com/support/framemaker.

Review questions

1 What does the Snap command do?

2 What is the difference between importing a graphic by copying it into the document and importing a graphic by reference?

3 Name an advantage of each method of importing graphics.

4 What is the function of the Tools palette?

5 What does the Group command do?

Review answers

1 The Snap command makes objects snap to an invisible grid as you draw, drag, or resize them.

2 Importing a copy of a graphic places a copy of the original graphic into the document. Importing a graphic by reference links the document to the original graphic.

3 When you import a graphic by copying, you can move the document without regard to the original source graphic. You can also modify, move, or delete the original graphic without affecting the image placed in the document. When you import by reference, you can greatly reduce the document's file size compared to importing the graphic by copying. Importing by reference also refreshes the graphics in the document whenever the original graphics are updated.

4 The Tools palette contains selection tools that control how you select text and objects, drawing tools for drawing various objects, and pop-up menus for changing an object's properties.

5 The Group command groups two or more objects into a single object. This makes it easier to move, modify, and copy the objects together.

6 USING ANCHORED GRAPHICS AND FRAMES

Lesson overview

In this lesson, you'll learn how to do the following:

- Import graphics into anchored frames

- Edit an anchored frame

- Change the position of an anchored frame

- Copy and reuse anchored frames

 This lesson takes approximately one hour to complete. If you have not already copied the resource files for this lesson onto your hard drive from the Lesson06 folder on the *Adobe FrameMaker 9 Classroom in a Book* CD, do so now. If needed, remove the previous lesson folder from your hard disk.

Chapter 10: Troubleshooting

No Power

There are only two reasons Modul9 will not turn on the instant you activate a panel: the batteries have not been installed or the batteries are dead. For information about the batteries, see "Installing the Batteries" on page 3.

Wireless Network Device Not Found

If you attempted to use the IP Wizard to **Automatically Detect and Assign** an IP address, it is possible that your wireless network device was not detected. Here are some things to try:

- Ensure your wireless device is turned on and connected to your network.
- Reboot your wireless device by pulling the power cord from the back of the device. Plug the device back in after 2 minutes and run the IP Wizard again.
- Perform a Soft Reset.

Resetting Modul9

There are two types of reset: **hard** and **soft**. Hard-resetting Modul9 will wipe out anything stored on your unit. You should only reset your unit if you would like to remove everything stored on the system. Soft-resetting will reboot the unit, which is sometimes necessary if the unit is no longer responding to your taps.

About anchored frames

You can draw illustrations in FrameMaker 9 or import them. If an illustration or object is intended to remain with particular document text, you place it in an *anchored frame* that's positioned in the column of text or in the page margin.

Each graphic in the practice document for this lesson is in an anchored frame; that is, a frame attached to the text. This means that when you edit the text, the frame and its graphic move with the text. This way, when adding or deleting text, the graphic stays near its related text.

Importing a graphic into an anchored frame

To begin this lesson, you will import a graphic.

1 Choose File > Open, and navigate to and open troubleshooting.fm in the Lesson06 folder.

2 Use the Go To Next Page and Go To Previous Page buttons in the status bar to page through the two-page document.

You will now import a graphic onto the first page of the document.

3 Go back to the first page.

4 Click in the text frame, at the end of the paragraph under the heading Resetting Modul9.

5 Press Enter once to begin a new line.

6 Choose File > Import > File.

7 In the Lesson06 folder, choose modul9cube.tif. Be sure Import By Reference is chosen and click Import.

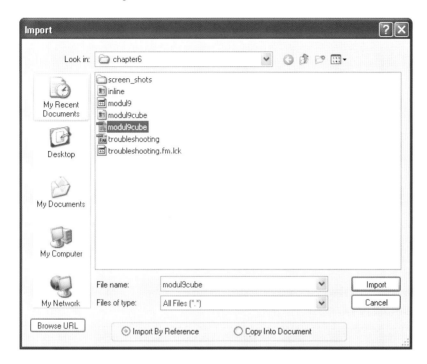

In the Import Graphic Scaling dialog box, be sure 72 dpi is chosen.

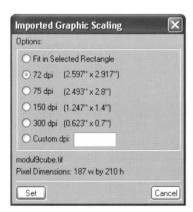

The graphic is now imported into an anchored frame. You will see two dotted frames around the image. The inside frame is the graphic's bounding box, and the outside frame represents the anchored frame. Initially, handles appear around the anchored frame, indicating that it is selected. Also, an anchor symbol (⊥) appears at the insertion point, if your text symbols are turned on.

Because there is not enough space left on the first page to display the graphic, it automatically jumps to page two of the document. You will add extra content above the graphic, to see how it stays with the text.

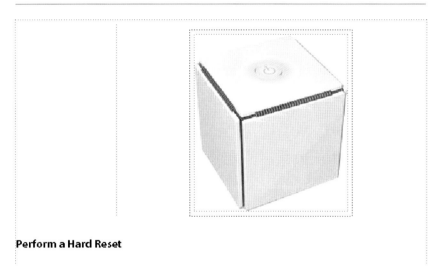

TROUBLESHOOTING
RESETTING MODUL9

Perform a Hard Reset

8   Click at the beginning of the empty paragraph containing the anchored frame, and press Enter three times. Notice how the text reflows and the graphic flows with it.

9   Remove the extra paragraph returns you just added by pressing Delete three times.

Editing anchored frames

Anchored frames act much like graphic frames. They can be resized, and their position can be adjusted to suit the situation—even outside of the column of text. FrameMaker 9 allows you the option to position your anchored frame in a variety of ways, and still enable it to flow with the text.

Resizing an anchored frame

The graphic is too large to fit onto page one, so you will resize the graphic and its anchored frame.

Notice there are two dotted lines surrounding the graphic. The inside line is the boundary of the graphic, and the outside line is the anchored frame and can help control the distance that the text will be offset from the graphic. This is also similar to what you would see if you had placed the graphic in a graphic frame (using the graphic frame tool instead of the anchored frame tool).

You will resize the graphic first, and then adjust its container, the outside line.

1 Click on the inside dotted line to select the graphic container. You will see handles on the edges of the graphic container.

2 Click the bottom-right corner handle.

3 Shift-drag the corner handle of the box up and to the left to decrease the size of the graphic.

4 Click on (or slightly outside) the outer dotted line; now you will see handles on this anchored frame rather than the handles from the graphic.

Note: If you had previously changed the relationship between the graphic and its frame, you may need to reposition the graphic to view the selection points.

Note: Holding down the Shift key as you drag constrains the proportions of the graphic as you resize it, keeping it from becoming distorted.

5 Click the bottom-right corner handle.

6 Drag the handle up and to the right, to resize the container to be just slightly larger than the graphic container.

7 Repeat this process if necessary, until the graphic appears on page one and is sized as shown here.

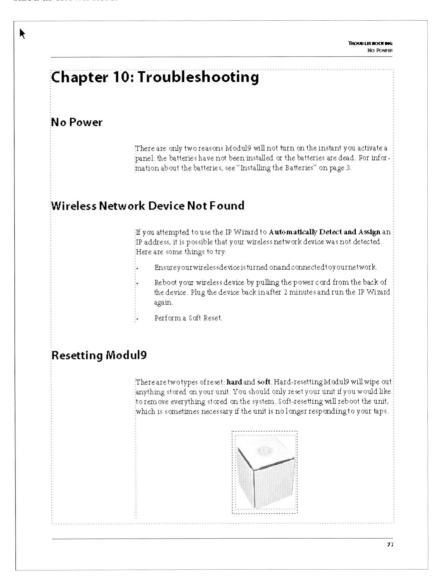

Notice the graphic is centered in the middle of the page. You will change its alignment next.

8 Click on (or slightly outside) the outer dotted line to select the anchored frame.

9 If the Anchored Frame panel is not visible, choose Special > Anchored Frame.

10 Choose Left from the Alignment menu in the middle of the panel.

▶ **Tip:** You can also click the Anchored Frame icon () in the Quick Access Bar near the top of the window.

11 Click Edit Frame.

The graphic has moved to the left side of the text frame. Notice the graphic is still anchored within the body text.

Anchoring graphics at the bottom of the column

You'll change the position of the graphic to appear at the bottom of the column.

1 Click the outside dotted line of the graphic frame.

2 In the Anchored Frame panel, click the arrow next to the Anchoring Position option, and choose At Bottom Of Column.

3 Click Edit Frame.

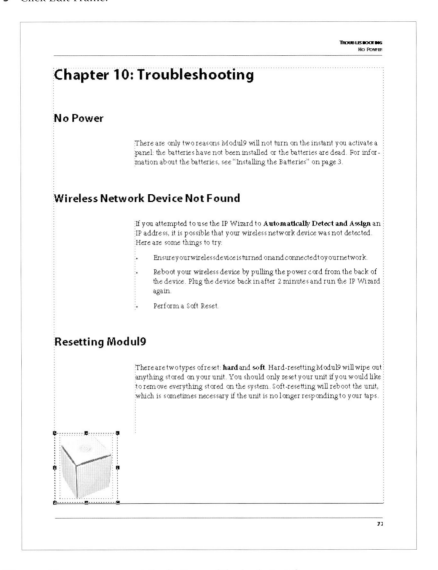

The graphic now appears at the bottom of the body text frame.

Positioning an anchored frame outside the column

Next, you will position the anchored frame outside the body text, so it appears in the margin, with more visual connection to the Resetting Modul9 heading.

1 Click the outer dotted line to select the graphic frame.

2 Click the arrow next to the Anchoring Position setting, and choose Outside Column.

3 Click Edit Frame.

The graphic now appears outside the column, but needs to be adjusted and pulled down. You will do that next.

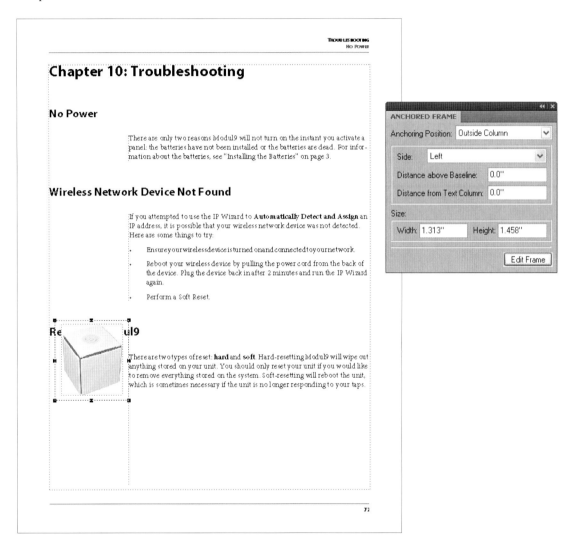

4 Click on the edge of the graphic frame to select it.

Note: Press Ctrl+L to redraw the display after a format edit or whenever you need to refresh the display.

5 Click on the graphic and drag straight down, until it clears the headline.

The graphic now appears in the left side of the document, under the Resetting Modul9 heading.

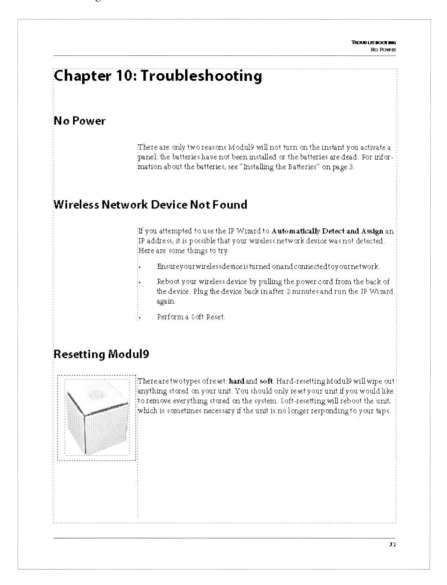

6 Choose File > Save.

Copying anchored frames

You'll use the same graphic on the second page of the document. You could import and position the graphic each time, but you can save time by copying and pasting the anchored frame and graphic.

1 With the anchored frame still selected, choose Edit > Copy.

2 Navigate to page two of the document, using the status bar Go To Next Page button.

3 Position the cursor at the end of the text on the second page.

4 Choose Edit > Paste. The copied graphic "inherits" the settings and position of the first one, so the graphic appears outside the column—already set appropriately, so you don't need to adjust the frame's position. (However, the two graphics are not otherwise connected to each other, so you can apply unique settings to any number of copies and not affect others.)

5 Press Ctrl+S to save your document.

Perform a Soft Reset

TASK
1. Turn Modul9 over.
2. Press and hold the upper left of the panel for 10 seconds. After 10 seconds, a message will appear on the back panel asking if you would like to continue.
3. Tap **Yes**.
4. Press and hold the lower left of the panel for 15 seconds. After 15 seconds, a message will appear on the back panel asking if you would like to **Soft Reset the Unit**.
5. Tap **Yes**. The system will turn itself off and back on.

Working with inline graphics

Inline graphics are small graphics that appear in a line of text. This book contains many inline graphics to help you identify tools and options. You will add a graphic to the first paragraph and format it to be an inline graphic.

1 Go to the first page of the document.

2 Click at the beginning of the first paragraph, just to the left of *There are only two reasons.*

3 Choose File > Import > File.

4 Select the Inline file in the folder called "Lesson06" (within the Lesson06 folder) and click Import.

5 In the Imported Graphic Scaling dialog box, select 150 dpi and click Set.

The graphic appears in an anchored frame within the paragraph.

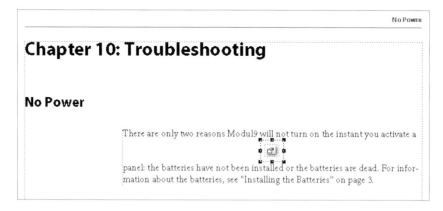

6   With the anchored frame still selected, press Esc+m+p. This is the shortcut for setting the Anchored Frame panel's Anchoring Position property to At Insertion Point. The anchored frame appears in the line of text, and the insertion point appears to the right of the anchored frame.

7   Press the spacebar to add a space between the frame and the inline graphic.

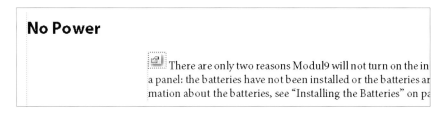

The graphic is sized correctly, but appears too high in the line.

8   Select the anchored frame (not the graphic).

You could drag the frame downward or use the arrow keys to reposition the frame, but you'll use the Anchored Frame panel this time.

9   If the Anchored Frame panel is not visible, choose Special > Anchored Frame.

10 Enter **-5** (type a hyphen, then the number five) in the Distance Above Baseline text box to move the frame down 5 points. Then click Edit Frame.

11 Save the file.

For more in-depth information on anchored frames and importing graphics, visit www.adobe.com/support/framemaker.

Review questions

1   What is an anchored frame? How is an anchored graphics frame useful?

2   Name three kinds of places a graphic can be positioned in a document.

3   What is a drop cap?

4   What does the Draw A Text Line tool do?

5   What is the shortcut for resizing a frame to fit a graphic and setting its position to At insertion point?

Review answers

1   An anchored frame is a frame that can contain a graphic or text frame and is anchored to the text. The frame and its contents move with the anchor, so you don't have to reposition the graphic or text when you edit the document.

2   Graphics can appear in several positions, including between words, between paragraphs, anchored to a spot in the text but positioned in the page margin, or relative to a spot on the page (such as at the top).

3   A drop cap is a large capital letter set into a piece of body text. It usually occurs at the beginning of a section of text.

4   The Draw A Text Line tool lets you create a single line of text that FrameMaker 9 treats independently from other text.

5   Esc+m+p.

7 EDITING DOCUMENTS

Lesson overview

In this lesson, you'll learn how to do the following:

- Hide the display of graphics in a document

- Define and insert user variables

- Change variable definitions

- Find and replace text

- Use the Thesaurus to find synonyms

- Find and correct spelling and typing errors

 This lesson takes approximately one hour to complete. If you have not already copied the resource files for this lesson onto your hard drive from the Lesson07 folder on the *Adobe FrameMaker 9 Classroom in a Book* CD, do so now. If needed, remove the previous lesson folder from your hard disk.

Chapter 5: Introducing the Cell Phone

Fold Modul9 so that three vertical squares are displayed and you've got yourself an ultra-thin cell phone. You'll appreciate the simplicity of the design.

The top square sports a large color video phone so you can see the person you're talking to; the bottom two squares present extra large buttons so dialing a call has never been easier. Driving? No problem. Your phone includes Hands-Free Voice Dialing. Simply say **Call**, mention anyone in your address book, and the phone quickly connects the call.

Figure 11: Cell Phone

Featuring:

- Color Video Phone
- Hands-Free Voice Dialing
- Large keypad buttons
- Up to 12 hours continuous digital talk time; up to 6 hours continuous analog talk time
- Modul9 Buddy Link Ready (Use your phone like a walkie-talkie; press one button and you can talk instantly with any Modul9 user on your Buddy List)
- HAC (Hearing Aid Compatible. Rating of M3 for hearing aids in the acoustic mode; T4 with hearing aids using telecoil)

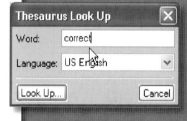

Thesaurus Look Up

Word: correct

Language: US English

Look Up...   Cancel

113

Getting started

FrameMaker's editing tools include the Find/Change command (for finding and changing not just text but other items as well), a spelling checker (which can find and correct misspelled words and common typing errors), and a thesaurus (which defines words and provides synonyms, antonyms, and related words). FrameMaker also offers a variety of user-defined varibles and supports the use of customizable variables, to streamline your workflow and make document-wide edits a simpler task. All of these various tools and features are designed to help save you time and ensure accuracy and efficiency.

Throughout this lesson, you'll explore ways to edit FrameMaker documents, and learn to disable graphics. You'll be working with the cellphone_GPS.fm file from the Lesson07 folder.

Hiding graphics

Throughout this lesson, and indeed most likely whenever you use FrameMaker, you'll select and edit text. To make pages display faster, and to make it easier to see the selected text, you can turn off the display of graphics.

with graphics displayed

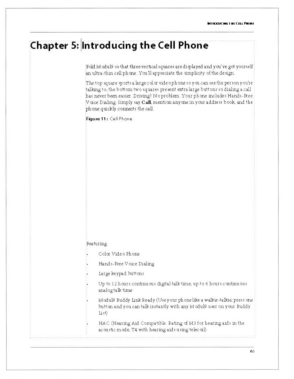

without graphics displayed

1   Open cellphone_GPS.fm in the Lesson07 folder.

2   Choose View > Options.

3   Deselect Graphics, and click Set.

The graphics disappear from the document. (They won't appear in print either.) They are not deleted—when you finish editing the text, you'll redisplay the graphics.

Creating and using variables

Variables allow you to reuse anything from plain text (product names, phone numbers) text to heavily formatted text (text-based logos with lots of font and color changes) in multiple locations across one or more files or books. To save typing and ensure consistency, you can use variables for words or phrases that appear in multiple places in a document.

Defining a user variable

A *user variable* is a placeholder for text, such as a technical term or a name, that you can define once and use repeatedly in a document. When you change the definition, FrameMaker 9 updates the instances of the variable throughout the document. In this way, variables can help save you time and ensure consistency in your documents.

In this part of the lesson, you'll create a user variable. You will define a variable for the long version of the Modul9's name, which appears frequently in the document.

First you'll define a user variable for the long name. Then you'll simply insert the variable rather than type the name yourself.

1   Select the term Modul9 in the first paragraph on the page.

Chapter 5: Introducing the Cell Phone

Fold Modul9 so that three vertical squares are displayed and you've got yourself an ultra-thin cell phone. You'll appreciate the simplicity of the design.

2   Click on the Variables Pod Tab to make it active.

The Variables pod opens, displaying a list of predefined variables.

3 Choose Create New User Variable (the second icon from the left).

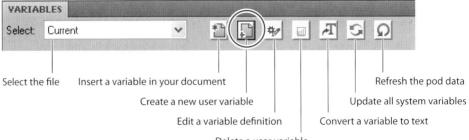

Select the file   Insert a variable in your document

Create a new user variable

Edit a variable definition

Delete a user variable

Refresh the pod data

Update all system variables

Convert a variable to text

The Add/Edit Variable panel appears.

4 Enter **LongName** in the Name text box, and enter **Modul9 Electronic All-In-One** in the Definition text box.

You could add a character format to the variable if, for instance, you wanted to add or change formatting applied to the text in the variable.

5 Click Add.

6 The new variable appears in the Variable pod.

You have created and saved a user variable and next, you will insert it into the document.

Inserting variables

Now you'll insert variables rather than type the text each time.

1 On page 1, double-click the word *Modul9* at the beginning of the fifth bulleted item to select the word.

2 From the Variables pod, in the Variables list, select LongName.

3 Click Insert (the first icon from the left on the Variables panel).

The selected text has been replaced by the LongName variable.

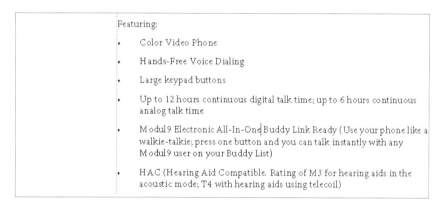

4 Click on the new text and notice that the entire phrase becomes highlighted, indicating it is indeed a variable. (Single-clicking within regular text would yield only a blinking text-insertion point.)

Now you'll insert another variable. This time, you'll use a keyboard shortcut.

5 In the status bar, click the Go To Next Page icon to display the second page of the document.

6 Select the word Modul9 in the second paragraph under the heading *Chapter 5: Overview of the GPS Panel.*

You'll never get lost again thanks to your Modul9 GPS system.

The GPS panel allows you to view your current geographic location anywhere in the world and is accurate within two feet. Once your location has been determined, you can plot a course from your current location to nearly any address or location in the world. You can create hot spots that mark any location. Once a hot spot has been defined, you can create **routes** and **tracks** on graphic maps stored with Modul9's memory module. You can then plot a course between any two hot spots.

✓ Not Applicable

Page Count
Current Date (Long)
Current Date (Short)
Modification Date (Long)
Modification Date (Short)
Creation Date (Long)
Creation Date (Short)
Filename (Long)
Filename (Short)
Table Continuation
Table Sheet
Volume Number
Chapter Number
Section Number
Sub Section Number
Chapter Title Name
LongName

---

7 Press Ctrl+0 (zero). A context menu appears and prompts you for a variable name.

8 Type the letter **L**. Because only the LongName variable begins with the letter *L*, the LongName variable is immediately added to the text.

● **Note:** If more than one variable exists with the same beginning letter, FrameMaker will highlight the first instance in the list, and you can scroll using your down arrow key to find the proper variable name.

Changing existing information

You are probably already familiar with Find/Change for locating and editing basic text information, but in FrameMaker the Find/Change helps you find nearly anything you've created within your FrameMaker file. If your file is part of a book, it will search across all the files in a book as well.

Finding and changing text

Because the article was typed before the LongName variable was defined, the short term *Modul9* still appears throughout the article as typed text rather than as a variable. You'll change that by replacing occurrences of *Modul9* throughout the document with the LongName variable.

1 Go back to page 1.

2 In the fifth bulleted item, click *Modul9 Electronic-All-In-One* once to select the variable. (If you double-click by mistake, the Variable dialog box appears. Just click Cancel.)

• Modul9 Electronic All-In-One Buddy Link Ready (Use your phone like walkie-talkie; press one button and you can talk instantly with any Modul9 user on your Buddy List)

3 Choose Edit > Copy. The variable is copied to the Clipboard.

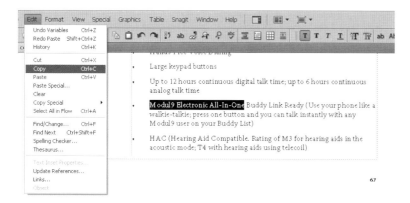

4 Make the Find/Change panel active. (If needed, choose Edit > Find/Change.)

5 Enter **Modul9** in the Find text box.

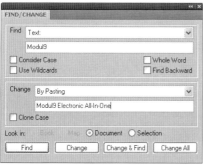

6 Choose By Pasting from the Change pop-up menu. This option lets you replace by pasting whatever you last copied—in this case, the LongName variable.

7 Click Find. The next occurrence of Modul9 on page 1 is selected.

8 Click Change & Find. The selected text is replaced with the variable, and the next occurrence is selected.

The article contains quite a few occurrences of the word Modul9, so you'll have FrameMaker 9 replace them all at the same time.

9   Make sure that Document is selected in the Look In: area near the bottom of the dialog box, click Change All, and then click OK.

All the remaining occurrences of the word Modul9 in this document are replaced by the LongName variable.

10 Close the Find/Change dialog box.

Finding text in other ways

You can use Find/Change and Find/Next commands to find many other items, not just text. For instance, you can choose Variable Of Name from the Find menu in the dialog box and type the name of the variable to find or change.

Or, you can specify a paragraph tag and its name to quickly find the next or previous instance of that paragraph format in your document.

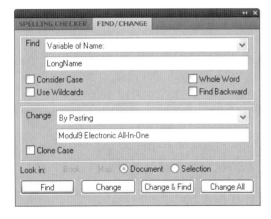 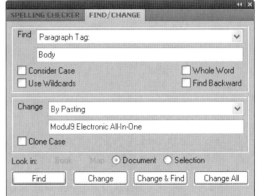

Changing a variable definition

FrameMaker 9 allows you to easily change a variable's definition. For example, if the product name changes, you will need to update it throughout the document. If you have used variables, you can easily change the definition. In addition, you can use the character formatting features to change the look of the variable content.

You'll change the definition for the LongName variable from *Modul9 Electronic All-In-One* to *M9*. FrameMaker 9 will then make the change throughout the document.

1   If the Variables pod is not still open, choose Special > Variables, and then choose Variables.

2   Select LongName in the Variables list.

Click the Edit icon at the top of the Variables panel. This opens the Add/Edit Variable panel.

3 In the Add/Edit Variable panel, replace the existing definition with M9 in the Definition field.

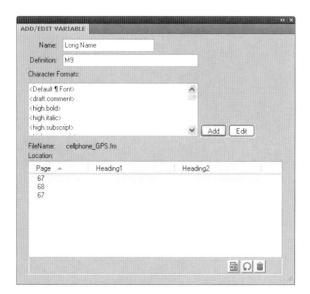

Note: You can also import variable definitions from other FrameMaker documents using the File > Import > Formats command. This is a useful way to ensure consistency in a family of documents.

4 Click Edit.

Thesaurus and Spelling Checker

Of course no chapter on editing documents would be complete without information on checking spelling and other tools for working with words.

Using the Thesaurus

The FrameMaker 9 Thesaurus provides you with alternate words that have a similar meaning to a selected word. In this part of the lesson, you'll replace the word *accurate* with a synonym from the Thesaurus.

1 Go back to the second page of the document, and double-click the word *accurate* in the second paragraph.

> The GPS panel allows you to view your current geographic location anywhere in the world and is **accurate** within two feet. Once your location has been determined, you can plot a course from your current location to nearly any address or location in the world. You can create hot spots that mark any location. Once a hot spot has been defined, you can create **routes** and **tracks** on graphic maps stored with Modul9 Electronic All-In-One's memory module. You can then plot a course between any two hot spots.

2 Choose Edit > Thesaurus.

The Thesaurus dialog box appears. It contains several definitions for *accurate* and a list of synonyms for each definition.

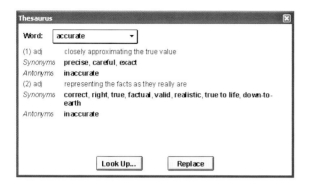

3 Click the word *precise* in the first Synonyms list. The Thesaurus dialog box now contains the definition and synonyms for *precise*.

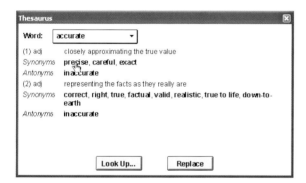

Before you decide to use *precise*, you'll try a word of your own.

4 Click Look Up. The Thesaurus Look Up dialog box appears.

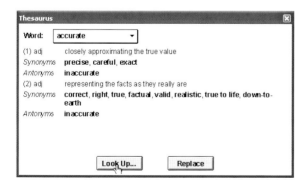

5   Enter **correct** in the Word text box and, click Look Up.

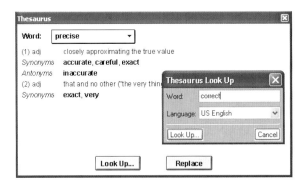

6   The Thesaurus dialog box now contains the definition and synonyms for *correct*.

Unfortunately, *correct* doesn't seem close enough to the meaning you intend.

7   In the Thesaurus dialog box, choose *precise* from the Word menu. (The words you've recently looked up appear in the menu.)

Note: If the Thesaurus dialog box is hidden by the document window, choose Edit > Thesaurus.

8   Click Replace.

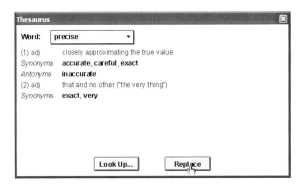

The GPS panel allows you to view your current geographic location anywhere in the world and is precise within two feet. Once your location has been determined, you can plot a course from your current location to nearly any address or location in the world. You can create hot spots that mark any location. Once a hot spot has been defined, you can create **routes** and **tracks** on graphic maps stored with Modul9 Electronic All-In-One's memory module. You can then plot a course between any two hot spots.

These are panels and do not need to be closed.

Checking spelling

You're almost finished with the article, so you'll check the spelling next.

1 Go back to page 1.

2 Click in the heading *Chapter 5* to place the insertion point.

Chapter 5: Overview of the GPS Panel

3 Choose Edit > Spelling Checker...

4 Click Start Checking.

Because the first word found—*quickley*—is not in any of the dictionaries, FrameMaker 9 selects the word and suggests that it's a misspelling. FrameMaker 9 recommends a spelling of *quick ley*, and provides several other choices.

The suggested correction is not the right one, so you'll choose from the list below.

5 Click **quickly**.

Next, FrameMaker 9 stops at the repeated words *of of* and suggests that only one of the words is necessary. This is a typing error, of course, rather than a spelling error.

6 Click Correct.

7 Click Start Checking again.

FrameMaker 9 stops on the word **walkie**. Since this is a word you may wish to use again, you want FrameMaker to allow this word.

8 Click Learn. This feature will allow you to add this word or phrase to your dictionary for future use.

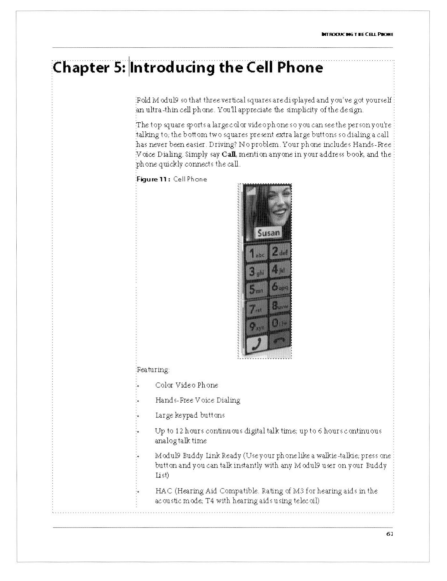

Chapter 5: Introducing the Cell Phone

Fold Modul9 so that three vertical squares are displayed and you've got yourself an ultra-thin cell phone. You'll appreciate the simplicity of the design.

The top square sports a large color videophone so you can see the person you're talking to; the bottom two squares present extra large buttons so dialing a call has never been easier. Driving? No problem. Your phone includes Hands-Free Voice Dialing. Simply say **Call**, mention anyone in your address book, and the phone quickly connects the call.

Figure 11: Cell Phone

Featuring:

- Color Video Phone
- Hands-Free Voice Dialing
- Large keypad buttons
- Up to 12 hours continuous digital talk time; up to 6 hours continuous analog talk time
- Modul9 Buddy Link Ready (Use your phone like a walkie-talkie; press one button and you can talk instantly with any Modul9 user on your Buddy List)
- HAC (Hearing Aid Compatible. Rating of M3 for hearing aids in the acoustic mode; T4 with hearing aids using telecoil)

63

Save and close the document.

For more in-depth information on variables, the Find/Change, Spelling Checker, and Thesaurus commands, visit www.adobe.com/support/framemaker.

Customizable dictionary options

FrameMaker uses three kinds of dictionaries:

- The **main dictionary** contains words found in a standard dictionary. You can't add or delete words in this dictionary.

- A **personal dictionary** contains words that aren't in the main dictionary but that you want FrameMaker 9 to allow when it checks any document on your computer. You can add and delete words in this dictionary. You can save multiple dictionaries for use with different projects.

- A **document dictionary** contains words that FrameMaker 9 allows in the current document, but that aren't found in the main or personal dictionaries. Unlike the other two dictionaries, the document dictionary isn't a separate file; it's actually part of the document. You can add and delete words in the document dictionary.

Review questions

1 Why might you turn off graphics when editing a document? How do you hide and display graphics?

2 What is a variable? Why should you use one?

3 How do you create a variable?

4 What does the Thesaurus do? How do you open it?

Review answers

1 Hiding graphics makes pages display faster, which can make it easier to edit text. To hide or display graphics, choose View > Options, select or deselect Graphics, and click Set.

2 A variable is a placeholder for text. Once you define a variable—such as with a product name or term—that text appears wherever you insert the variable in your document. If you change the definition later, FrameMaker 9 updates all occurrences of that variable in the document with the updated text. By changing the variable's definition, you don't have to retype or find and replace each occurrence of text you want to reuse. You also ensure that the text is used consistently in the document.

3 To create a variable, select the text you want to use, choose Special > Variables, and then click Create A New User Variable. Enter a name for the variable in the Name text box, and enter the variable text and character format(s) in the Definition text box. Click Add, and then click Done. When the new variable appears in the Variable dialog box, click Done.

4 You use the Thesaurus to look up words with a similar meaning to the word you specify. To open the Thesaurus, choose Edit > Thesaurus.

8 FORMATTING TABLES

Lesson overview

In this lesson, you'll learn how to do the following:

- Insert an empty table

- Fill in the contents of a table

- Add rows and columns to a table

- Resize columns

- Rearrange rows and columns

- Change a table format

 This lesson takes approximately 30 minutes to complete. If you have not already copied the resource files for this lesson onto your hard drive from the Lesson08 folder on the *Adobe FrameMaker 9 Classroom in a Book* CD, do so now. If needed, remove the previous lesson folder from your hard disk.

Chapter 7: Introducing the Digital Camera

Fold Module so that three horizontal squares are displayed and you've got yourself a digital camera with some bells and whistles you wouldn't expect in such a tiny unit.

Figure 13: Digital Camera

Not only will you be able to capture fantastic images at up to 12 megapixels, but the resulting images can be resized up to a whopping 20 × 30 inches.

The camera includes the following features:

Camera Features and Specifications	
Lens	23 mm-fixed, 6X zoom: 39–3277 mm
Shutter speed	6–1/1448 sec
LCD	high resolution (430kb pixels)
Color display	6 level indoor/outdoor brightness adjustment
ISO sensitivity	auto: 50 –200; manual: 50, 100, 200, 400, 800, 1000
Compression	JPEG

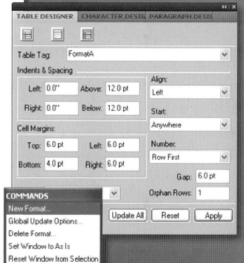

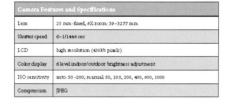

Table basics

You can use tables to organize information and to make it attractive and easy to understand. New FrameMaker 9 documents contain built-in table formats that determine the appearance of tables. You can customize and store table formats in a document's Table Designer or import them from a template and reuse them as needed.

Like paragraph and character formats, table formats are stored in a catalog. However, unlike Paragraph formats and Character formats, Table formats appear only in the Table Designer and in the scroll list in the Insert Table dialog box rather than in a palette, as you'll soon see.

Tables can have titles, heading rows, footing rows, and body rows. Heading rows might be set up with categories for the table data. Body rows are typically where the bulk of the information is stored. Footing rows are for items you wish to display at the bottom of the table. If your table runs long and extends to another page, the heading and footing rows automatically repeat, along with the table title (if any), on subsequent pages.

The document you will open has an existing formatted table. You will create another table and format it.

Inserting a table

For starters, you'll create a small table that lists different model numbers and external case colors for the Modul9.

1   Open camera.fm in the Lesson08 folder.

2   Choose File > Save As, enter the filename **camera1.fm**, and click Save.

3   Look at the Page Status area in the status bar.

4   The first page of the document is visible.

5   Choose View > Text Symbols to display the text symbols, if they are not currently turned on.

6 Click in the empty paragraph below the table.

7 Press Enter twice. You will see two new paragraph symbols.

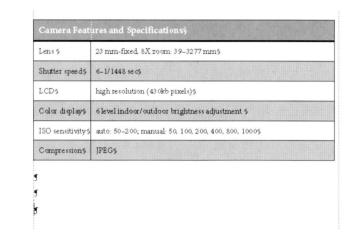

8 Choose Table > Insert Table.

The table catalog for this document contains eight table formats, among them Format A and Format B.

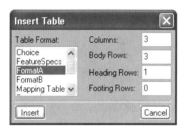

⬤ **Note:** You cannot view the Table Catalog as you would the Paragraph and Character catalogs. One way to view the available table formats is to open the Table Designer.

9 Select Format A in the Table Format scroll list.

The table format controls the appearance of the table, but you still need to choose how large the table will be.

10 Enter **3** in the Columns text field, **3** in the Body Rows text field, and **1** in the Heading Rows text field. You'll eventually need another column and another row, but you'll add them later.

11 Click Insert. The table's *anchor symbol* (⊥) appears where the insertion point was, and the new empty table appears below the paragraph symbol. The anchor connects the table to the text, so that when you edit the text, the anchor and the table move with it.

Camera Features and Specifications§	
Lens §	23 mm-fixed, 8X zoom: 39–327.7 mm§
Shutter speed§	6–1/1448 sec§
LCD§	high resolution (430kb pixels)§
Color display§	6 level indoor/outdoor brightness adjustment §
ISO sensitivity§	auto: 50–200; manual: 50, 100, 200, 400, 800, 1000§
Compression§	JPEG§

⊥

§	§	§
§	§	§

Filling in the table

Now you'll fill in the heading row and the body rows.

1 Click in the first heading cell and type **Model No**.

2 Press Tab, type **Case Color**, press Tab again, type **Price**, and press Tab again.

The heading row is complete, and the first body cell is highlighted.

▷ **Tip:** To move back one cell, press Shift+Tab.

Model No.§	Case Color§	Price§
§	§	§
§	§	§
§	§	§

3 Type **M9-646A**, press Tab, type **Silver**, press Tab, type **699.99**, and press Tab again to complete the first body row.

Model No.§	Case Color§	Price§
M9-646A§	Silver§	699.95§
███§	§	§
§	§	§

4 Fill in the remaining body rows with data to match the image of the finished table below.

Model No.§	Case Color§	Price§
M9-646A§	Silver§	699.99§
M9-677A§	Black§	599.95§
M9-698A§	White§	499.99§

> **Note:** To move up or down one row in the same column, press Ctrl+Alt+Tab or Ctrl+Alt+Shift+Tab.

Adding rows and columns

The table needs another row for a new Modul9 model and another column for the availability. First you'll add a row.

1 With the insertion point in the last row of the table, press Ctrl+Enter. An empty row is inserted below the insertion point.

Model No.§	Case Color§	Price§
M9-646A§	Silver§	699.95§
M9-677A§	Black§	599.95§
M9-698A§	White§	499.99§
§	§	§

2 Type **M9-543A**, press Tab, type **Magenta,** press Tab, and type **399.99**.

Model No.§	Case Color§	Price§
M9-646A§	Silver§	699.99§
M9-677A§	Black§	599.95§
M9-698A§	White§	499.99§
M9-543A§	Magenta§	399.99§

Now you'll add a column.

Tip: The Quick Access Bar contains some commonly used commands for editing tables. To display the Quick Access Bar, choose View > Toolbars > Quick Access Bar.

3 With the insertion point still in the last column, right-click, and then choose Table > Add Rows Or Columns.

4 Select Add 1 Column, choose Right Of Selection from the menu, and click Add.

A fourth column appears at the right side of the table.

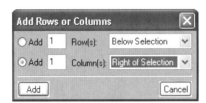

5 Click in the empty heading cell at the top of the new column, and type **Availability**.

Model No.§	Case Color§	Price§	Availability§
M9-646A§	Silver§	699.95§	§
M9-677A§	Black§	599.95§	§
M9-698A§	White§	499.99§	§
§	§	§	§

6 Add dates in the new column.

Model No.§	Case Color§	Price§	Availability§
M9-646A§	Silver§	699.99§	Oct. 2009§
M9-677A§	Black§	599.95§	Nov. 2009§
M9-698A§	White§	499.99§	Jan. 2010§
M9-543A§	Magenta§	399.99§	Mar. 2010§

7 Save the document.

Modifying table information

There are many controls and features in FrameMaker that make it easy to modify, format, and arrange the content of tables.

Rearranging information

In this section, you will rearrange some of the information in the table. You'll move the Case Color column to the far right, and then move the Magenta row to the top of the table.

First, you'll move the column.

1 Drag from the heading Case Color down into the first body row to select the entire column.

▶ **Tip:** Whenever you drag from the heading into the body, the entire column is selected.

Model No.§	Case Color§	Price§	Availability§
M9-646A§	Silver§	699.99§	Oct. 2009§
M9-677A§	Black§	599.95§	Nov. 2009§
M9-698A§	White§	499.99§	Jan. 2010§
M9-543A§	Magenta§	399.99§	Mar. 2010§

2 Right-click, and choose Cut.

◉ **Note:** A complete list of keyboard shortcuts for Adobe FrameMaker 9 is available in Adobe Framemaker 9 Community Help by choosing Help > Framemaker Help.

Note: If the
screen display needs
redrawing, press Ctrl+l
(lowercase L).

3 In the Cut Table Cells dialog box, select Remove Cells From Table, and click
Cut.

The column of cells has been removed from the table.

4 Click anywhere in the last column of the table.

5 Right-click again, and choose Paste.

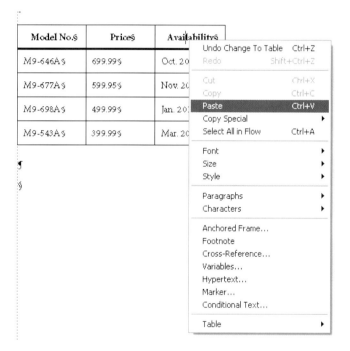

6 Select Insert Right Of Current Columns, and click Paste.

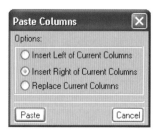

Model No.§	Price§	Availability§	Case Color§
M9-646A§	699.99§	Oct. 2009§	Silver§
M9-677A§	599.95§	Nov. 2009§	Black§
M9-698A§	499.99§	Jan. 2010§	White§
M9-543A§	399.99§	Mar. 2010§	Magenta§

Now you will move the Magenta row to the top of the table, just under the heading row.

7 Click in the last row, beginning with *M9-543A*, and drag to the right to select the entire row.

Model No.§	Price§	Availability§	Case Color§
M9-646A§	699.99§	Oct. 2009§	Silver§
M9-677A§	599.95§	Nov. 2009§	Black§
M9-698A§	499.99§	Jan. 2010§	White§
M9-543A§	399.99§	Mar. 2010§	Magenta§

8 Choose Edit > Cut, select Remove Cells From Table, and click Cut.

9 Click anywhere in the first body row, and choose Edit > Paste.

Note: To select a single cell, you can Ctrl-click the cell. Notice that the cursor changes into a resizing arrow (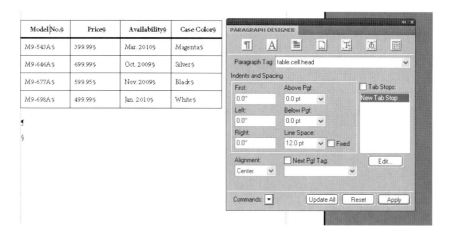) when it rolls over the selection handle, which appears on the cell's right edge at its middle vertical point.

10 Choose Insert Above Current Row, and click OK.

Model No.§	Price§	Availability§	Case Color§
M9-543A§	399.99§	Mar. 2010§	Magenta§
M9-646A§	699.99§	Oct. 2009§	Silver§
M9-677A§	599.95§	Nov. 2009§	Black§
M9-698A§	499.99§	Jan. 2010§	White§

Formatting text in table cells

When inserting a new table, its cells use a predetermined paragraph format stored within the table format. To change the text formatting in the table, you can change the paragraph formats applied to the content. You'll begin formatting the table by changing the table text to a smaller font.

1 Select any text in the heading row, and make the Paragraph Designer panel active. If needed, choose Format > Paragraphs > Designer. You'll see that the paragraphs in the heading cells use the table.cell.head paragraph format. (You can also see this information in the Tag area of the status bar.)

2 Click the Default Font icon at the top of the Paragraph Designer.

3 Change the Family to Myriad Pro, the Size to 8, and the Weight to Bold.

4 Click Update All.

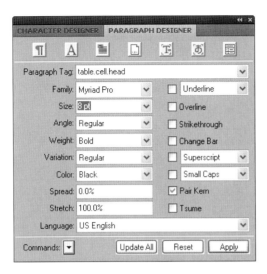

5 If the table headings appear as gray bars, click the Increase Zoom button (plus sign) in the status bar until the headings are legible.

You're finished with the heading format for now.

6 Click the text in any body cell. The paragraphs in body cells use the table.cell. body paragraph format.

7 In the Paragraph Designer, change the Family to Myriad Pro and the Size to 8, and then click Update All.

Finally, you'll center the numbers in the Price column of the table. Because you don't want to center the contents of all the body cells, you'll create a new paragraph format just for the centered body cells.

8 Drag to select all the body cells in the Price column.

Model No.§	Price§	Availability§	Case Color§
M9-646A§	699.99§	▪ Oct. 2009§	Silver§
M9-677A§	599.95§	▪ Nov. 2009§	Black§
M9-698A§	499.99§	▪ Jan. 2010§	White§
M9-543A§	399.99§	▪ Mar. 2010§	Magenta§

9 Click the Basic icon at the top of the Paragraph Designer.

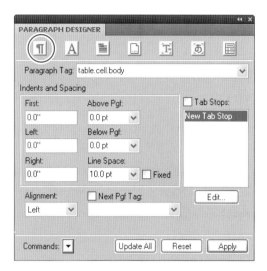

10 Choose Center from the Alignment menu, and click Apply.

The text in these cells is centered. Now you'll store this style as a new format.

Model No.§	Price§	Availability§	Case Color§
M9-543A§	399.99§	Mar. 2010§	Magenta§
M9-646A§	699.99§	Oct. 2009§	Silver§
M9-677A§	599.95§	Nov. 2009§	Black§
M9-698A§	499.99§	Jan. 2010§	White§

11 Choose New Format from the Commands menu at the bottom of the Paragraph Designer.

12 Enter **Price** in the Tag text box.

13 Make sure that both options—Store In Catalog and Apply To Selection—are selected, and click Create.

The current paragraph's tag changes and the Price format is added to the Paragraph Catalog.

14 Close the Paragraph Designer.

15 Save the document.

Changing table structure and appearance

You've seen some of the ways you can easily move and format table data, but you can also customize the tables themselves.

Resizing columns

Now that the text formats are finished, you'll resize the columns.

1 Drag from the first cell in the Price column to the last to select all of the prices.

Model No.§	Price§	Availability§	Case Color§
M9-646A§	699.99§	▪ Oct. 2009§	Silver§
M9-677A§	599.95§	▪ Nov. 2009§	Black§
M9-698A§	499.99§	▪ Jan. 2010§	White§
M9-543A§	399.99§	▪ Mar. 2010§	Magenta§

2 Drag the cell selection handle to the left slightly. All cells in the selected column are resized to match.

▶ **Tip:** You can quickly resize a column by placing the insertion point in a cell that has the desired column width of text and pressing Esc +t+w.

3 Repeat the resizing process with the Case Color column.

Model No.§	Price§	Availability§	Case Color§
M9-646A§	699.99§	Oct. 2009§	Silver§
M9-677A§	599.95§	Nov. 2009§	Black§
M9-698A§	499.99§	Jan. 2010§	White§
M9-543A§	399.99§	Mar. 2010§	Magenta§

4 Save the document.

Formatting a row

When you are using tables, and text reflows, the table can be split onto two pages, which may not be the best way to display the table. Next, you'll learn how to control where a table breaks, if at all.

In this example, you will also learn to use the contextual table menu items.

1 Navigate to the first page of the document, to the Camera Features and Specifications table.

2 Ctrl+click on the last cell in the first column, which reads Compressions.

3 Hold down and drag to the right to select the entire row.

4 Right-click to see the context menu, and choose Row Format.

5 Under the Keep With section, choose Previous Row.

Now, if the table breaks, you won't have a single row on the next page. It will be forced to stay with the previous row.

6 Save your work and close the file.

For in-depth information about tables, visit www.adobe.com/support/framemaker.

Review questions

1 Where are table formats stored?

2 Name four components that make up a table in FrameMaker 9.

3 What two keyboard shortcuts let you move forward and backward between cells?

4 What's the quickest way to insert an empty row below an insertion point?

5 How do you add a row or column?

6 How do you select a cell?

Review answers

1 As with paragraph and character formats, table formats are stored in a catalog (the Table Designer). The Table Designer appears in a scroll list in the Insert Table dialog box.

2 FrameMaker 9 tables include such elements as a title, rows, columns, heading rows, heading cells, body rows, body cells, rules, and shading.

3 To move forward one cell using the keyboard, press Tab. To move backward one cell using the keyboard, press Shift+Tab.

4 To insert an empty row below the insertion point, press Ctrl+Enter.

5 To add a row or column, click in a cell to set the insertion point. Choose Table > Add Rows Or Columns. Specify which you want, and how many. Then choose where you want the rows or columns to be located in relation to the insertion point, and click Add.

6 To select a cell using the mouse, drag from inside the cell through the border of the next cell and then back again to select just the one cell. You can also Ctrl-click the cell (Windows and UNIX) or Option-click it (Macintosh).

9 CUSTOMIZING TABLES

Lesson overview

In this lesson, you'll learn how to do the following:

- Import text into a table

- Change the paragraph format of table text

- Format body cells

- Indent text within table cells

- Apply custom ruling and shading to a table

- Creating custom formats and modifying table formats

You'll also use some of the skills you learned in the previous lesson to move information in a table, resize columns, and set up a table's basic design.

 This lesson takes approximately one hour to complete. If you have not already copied the resource files for this lesson onto your hard drive from the Lesson09 folder on the *Adobe FrameMaker 9 Classroom in a Book* CD, do so now. If needed, remove the previous lesson folder from your hard disk.

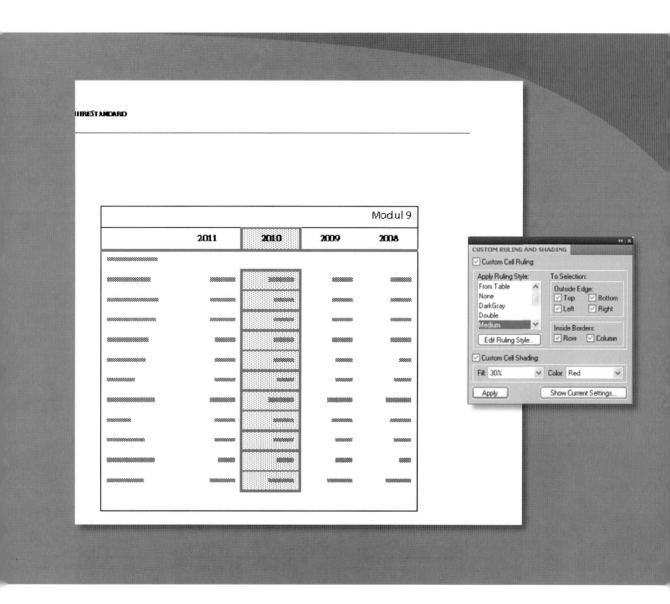

Getting started

Beyond typing data into tables, you can also import information from external sources.

During this lesson, you'll import financial data as a table into an annual report and then format the table.

1 Open welcome_formatted.fm in the Lesson09 folder.

2 Navigate to page 2.

You'll recreate the table that appears at the top of page 2.

Much of the table's appearance is determined by the table format. For example, the rules around the edge of the table and the rule separating the heading cells from the body of the table are specified in the table format. However, the thin rules that extend only partway across two of the rows and the shading for the third column are specified as custom ruling and shading properties for specific parts of the table. Custom ruling and shading are not contained in the table format; rather they are overrides of the format.

3 If you've opened welcome_formatted.fm to look at the completed table, close it now. If prompted to save changes, click No.

Importing text into a table

First you'll import some financial data into a table.

1 Open welcome.fm in the Lesson09 folder.

2 Choose File > Save As, enter the filename **welcome2.fm**, and click Save.

Page 2 of the welcome document is empty, and you will now insert a page break to allow the new table you create to start at the top of page 2.

3 Click at the end of the last paragraph on the first page and add a paragraph return.

4 Right-click and choose Page Break.

5 In the Page Break dialog box, choose At Top Of Next Available Page, and click Set.

Your cursor now rests at the top of page 2.

6 Choose File > Import > File.

7 Select Modul9Sales.txt in the Lesson09 folder.

8 Select Copy Into Document, and then click Import.

Note: Online Help provides additional information on file types and filters.

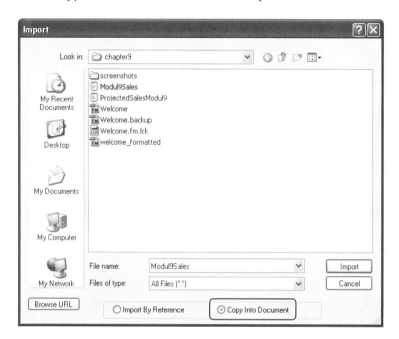

9 If the Unknown File Type dialog box appears, select Text in the scroll list, and click Convert.

10 In the Import Text File By Copy dialog box, select Convert Text To Table. The Encoding menu selects the appropriate option.

11 Click Import.

No table format has been set up for financial data, so you'll use one of the default table formats and then modify it later.

12 Select FormatA in the Table Format scroll list.

The data is stored as tab-delimited text—that is, each paragraph represents a row of the table, and tabs separate the contents of one cell from another.

13 In the Treat Each Paragraph As area, make sure these options are selected: A Row With Cells Separated By, and Tabs. Then enter **2** in the Heading Rows text box.

14 Click Convert.

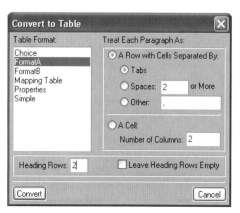

Note: In the next several steps, you'll change the paragraph formats of table cells. This part of the lesson extends the type of formatting you did in "Formatting text in table cells" in Lesson 8, "Formatting Tables."

15 In the next dialog box, click OK to continue.

The imported information appears in a table.

Modul9				
	2011	**2010**	**2009**	**2008**
Projected Sales:				
United States	203,461	146,992	89,557	72,429
Western Europe	157,700	90,853	55,650	47,005
Eastern Europe	101,006	72,448	35,543	30,451
Western Asia	49,349	30,557	20,512	15,627
Eastern Asia	32,544	12,953	6,430	350
Australia	12,542	9,600	5,398	3,213
South America	556,602	363,403	213,090	169,075
Canada	35,601	51,525	42,508	12,954
Philippines	20,428	10,327	6,972	3,451
Southeast Asia	3,655	2,153	1,078	446
Total assets	616,286	427,408	263,648	185,921

Formatting the imported table data

Next, you'll create new Table Formats for the table headings, and then save them as paragraph formats.

1 Click in the heading cell that contains the word Modul9, and notice the style saved is table.cell.head.

2 Choose Format > Paragraphs > Designer.

3 Click the Default Font icon.

4 Change the Family to Myriad Pro.

5 Click Update All.

6 If necessary, click the Zoom In button (plus sign) in the status bar until you can read the headings easily.

Now you'll move the heading Modul9 to the right side of the table.

7 Drag from inside the cell that contains the text Modul9 through the border of the next cell and then back again to select just the one cell. (You can tell that the cell is selected because the entire cell is highlighted, rather than just the text in it, and because a selection handle appears at the right side of the cell.)

▶ **Tip:** Another way to select the cell is to Ctrl-click the cell. This method can be easier for selecting single cells.

Modul9				
	2011	2010	2009	2008

8 Choose Edit > Cut, click in the rightmost cell in the row, and choose Edit > Paste. The heading is now in the rightmost cell.

				Modul9
	2011	2010	2009	2008

Now you'll make the heading right-aligned and in uppercase letters. To leave the other heading cells centered, you'll create a new paragraph format for this heading.

9 In the Paragraph Designer, choose Uppercase from the bottommost pop-up menu in the right-hand column.

10 Choose New Format from the Commands menu at the bottom of the Paragraph Designer.

11 Enter **CellHeadingRight** in the Tag text box.

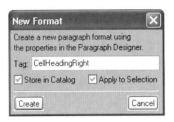

12 Make sure that both options—Store In Catalog and Apply To Selection—are selected, and click Create.

The current paragraph's tag changes to CellHeadingRight, and the CellHeadingRight format is added to the Paragraph Catalog.

13 In the Paragraph Designer, choose Basic from the Properties pop-up menu.

14 Choose Right from the Alignment pop-up menu. Then click Update All.

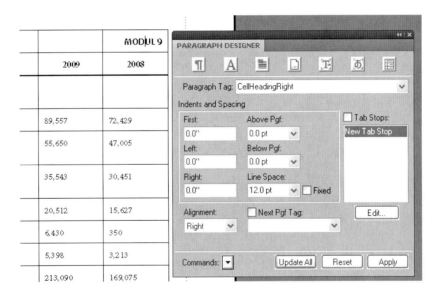

Formatting body cells

You'll need two paragraph formats for the body cells. The numbers (the basic body cells) will be right-aligned, but the row labels (the geographical areas) will be left-aligned and will contain tab stops. You'll set up both of these formats.

Row labels

1   Click in the first body cell (the cell that contains Projected Sales).

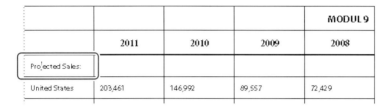

2   In the Paragraph Designer, click the Default Font icon.

3   Change the Family to Myriad Pro and the Size to 8, and click Update All.

4   Drag downward from the cell that contains the text *Projected Sales* until all the body cells in that column are selected.

5   In the Paragraph Designer, choose Basic from the Properties pop-up menu.

6   In the Tab Stops area, with New Tab Stop selected in the Tab Stops scroll list, click Edit.

7 Enter **10 pt** in the New Position text box. (Be sure to enter the **pt**, because you want the measurement to be in points.)

8 Make sure that the Alignment is set to Left and that the Leader is set to None. Then click Continue.

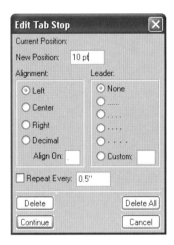

The tab stop appears in the Tab Stops scroll list.

9 With New Tab Stop selected in the Tab Stops scroll list, click Edit again.

10 Enter **20 pt** in the New Position text box, and click Continue. (Be sure to enter the **pt**, because you want the measurement to be in points.)

11 Choose New Format from the Commands pop-up menu.

12 Enter **RowLabel** in the Tag text box.

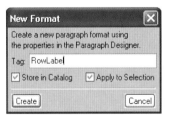

13 Make sure that both options—Store In Catalog and Apply To Selection—are selected. Then click Create.

The current paragraph's tag changes to RowLabel, and the RowLabel format is added to the Paragraph Catalog.

Body cells

Now you'll change the format for the remaining body cells.

1 Click in one of the body cells that contains a numerical value.

2 In the Paragraph Designer, choose Right from the Alignment menu, and click Update All.

	2011	2010	2009	MODUL 9 2008
Projected Sales:				
United States	203,461	146,992	89,557	72,429
Western Europe	157,700	90,853	55,650	47,005
Eastern Europe	101,006	72,448	35,543	30,451
Western Asia	49,349	30,557	20,512	15,627
Eastern Asia	32,544	12,953	6,430	350
Australia	12,542	9,600	5,398	3,213
South America	556,602	363,403	213,090	169,075
Canada	35,601	51,525	42,508	12,954
Philippines	20,428	10,327	6,972	3,451
Southeast Asia	3,655	2,153	1,078	446
Total assets	616,286	427,408	263,648	185,921

Setting basic table properties

Now you're ready to set overall table properties.

Spacing and cell margins

First you'll change the space above the table and its cell margins.

1 Make sure that the insertion point is in the table. If the Table Designer is not already open, open it by choosing Table > Table Designer.

2 Click the Basic icon at the top of the Table Designer.

3 In the Indents & Spacing area, change Above to **20**, and in the Cell Margins area, change Top to **4**.

Note: To redraw the screen if necessary, press Ctrl+l (lowercase letter L).

4 Click Update All.

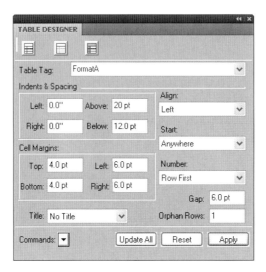

	2011	2010	2009	Model 9
				2008
Projected Sales:				
United States	203,461	146,992	89,557	72,429
Western Europe	157,700	90,853	55,650	47,005
Eastern Europe	101,006	72,448	35,543	30,451
Western Asia	49,349	30,557	20,512	15,627
Eastern Asia	32,544	12,953	6,430	350
Australia	12,542	9,600	5,398	3,213
South America	556,602	363,403	213,090	169,075
Canada	35,601	51,525	42,508	12,954
Philippines	20,428	10,327	6,972	3,451
Southeast Asia	3,655	2,153	1,078	446
Total assets	616,286	427,408	263,648	185,921

Resizing columns

In Lesson 8, you learned how to resize columns on the fly. Now you'll resize the table columns in a more precise way. To begin, you'll verify that the table is measured in points. (There are 72 points in an inch.)

1   Choose View > Options.

2   Make sure the Display Units menu is set to Point, and click Set.

3   Drag from the heading cell that contains the text *2011* to the rightmost heading cell. The four cells are selected.

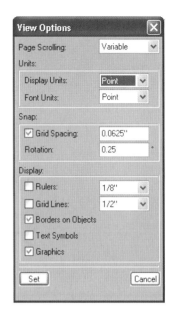

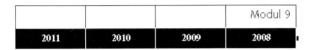

4   Choose Table > Resize Columns.

5   Enter **6** in the To Width text box, and then click Resize.

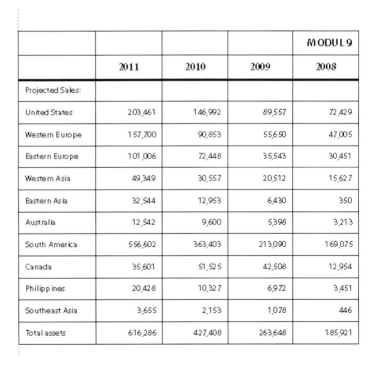

	2011	2010	2009	2008
				MODUL 9
Projected Sales:				
United States	203,461	146,992	89,557	72,429
Western Europe	157,700	90,853	55,650	47,005
Eastern Europe	101,006	72,448	35,543	30,451
Western Asia	49,349	30,557	20,512	15,627
Eastern Asia	32,544	12,953	6,430	350
Australia	12,542	9,600	5,398	3,213
South America	556,602	363,403	213,090	169,075
Canada	35,601	51,525	42,508	12,954
Philippines	20,428	10,327	6,972	3,451
Southeast Asia	3,655	2,153	1,078	446
Total assets	616,286	427,408	263,648	185,921

6 Drag to select several cells in the first column of the table.

7 Drag a selection handle to the right slightly to resize the column. You'll see that you don't have to have all of the cells in a column or row selected in order to resize the entire column or row.

Finally, you will resize the first column, to give it a little more space.

8 Select the column with Projected Sales.

9 Right-click and choose Resize Columns. Change the width of the column to 110.

10 Click Resize.

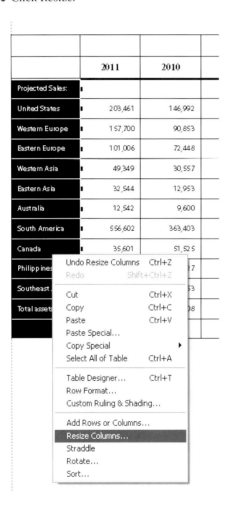

	2011	2010	2009	2008 MODUL 9
Projected Sales:				
United States	203,461	146,992	89,557	72,429
Western Europe	157,700	90,853	55,650	47,005
Eastern Europe	101,006	72,448	35,543	30,451
Western Asia	49,349	30,557	20,512	15,627
Eastern Asia	32,544	12,953	6,430	350
Australia	12,542	9,600	5,398	3,213
South America	556,602	363,403	213,090	169,075
Canada	35,601	51,525	42,508	12,954
Philippines	20,428	10,327	6,972	3,451
Southeast Asia	3,655	2,153	1,078	446
Total assets	616,286	427,408	263,648	185,921

11 Save your work.

Straddling cells

You can also make text straddle the cells you select. (Some programs refer to this process as "merging" or combining the cells.) Here you'll straddle two cells so that the heading fits on one line.

1 Drag to select the cell that contains the text Projected Sales and the four cells to its right.

2 Choose Table > Straddle.

The text now spans five cells.

	2011	2010	2009	2008 Modul 9
Projected Sales:				
United States	203,461	146,992	89,557	72,429

Working with titles

Adding a title to a table

You can add titles above or below a table, which will be repeated on all pages of a multi-page table. The table format determines the look of the table.

1   Click in the table and choose Table > Table Designer, if it is not already visible.

2   In the Basic properties of the Table Designer, choose Above Table from the Title options.

3   Set the gap to 12. Pt.

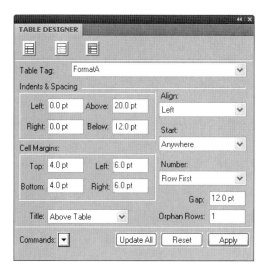

4   Click Update All.

A blank title appears above the table, with 12 points between it and the table.

Table 1:				
				MODUL 9
	2011	2010	2009	2008
Projected Sales:				
United States	203,461	146,992	89,557	72,429
Western Europe	157,700	90,853	55,650	47,005
Eastern Europe	101,006	72,448	35,543	30,451
Western Asia	49,349	30,557	20,512	15,627
Eastern Asia	32,544	12,953	6,430	350

5 Add **Projected Modul9 Sales by Region** after the table title.

Table 1: Projected Modul9 Sales by Region				MODUL 9
	2011	2010	2009	2008
Projected Sales:				
United States	203,461	146,992	89,557	72,429
Western Europe	157,700	90,853	55,650	47,005
Eastern Europe	101,006	72,448	35,543	30,451
Western Asia	49,349	30,557	20,512	15,627
Eastern Asia	32,544	12,953	6,430	350
Australia	12,542	9,600	5,398	3,213
South America	556,602	363,403	213,090	169,075
Canada	35,601	51,525	42,508	12,954
Philippines	20,428	10,327	6,972	3,451
Southeast Asia	3,655	2,153	1,078	446
Total assets	616,286	427,408	263,648	185,921

Deleting a table's title

Next, you will learn how to delete a title from a table.

1 Click in the table.

2 In the Table Designer, choose No Title from the Title Options.

3 Click Update All.

				MODUL 9
	2011	2010	2009	2008
Projected Sales:				
United States	203,461	146,992	89,557	72,429
Western Europe	157,700	90,853	55,650	47,005
Eastern Europe	101,006	72,448	35,543	30,451
Western Asia	49,349	30,557	20,512	15,627

4 Save your work.

Ruling styles

Custom ruling within tables can be saved with the table format, to create a custom look that can be reapplied to other tables. In this exercise, you will create a custom ruling style.

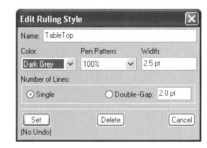

Defining ruling styles

To make the table appear with custom ruling, you will create a ruling style.

1   Choose Table > Custom Ruling & Shading. The available ruling styles appear in the Apply Ruling Style list.

2   Select Medium in the Apply Ruling Style list, and click Edit Ruling Style.

3   Type **TableTop** in the Name area. Change the Color to **Red** and the Width to **2.5** points. Click Set and then click Continue.

4   Save the file.

Fine-tuning table ruling

Now you're ready to fine-tune the table ruling.

1   Choose View > Borders to hide the borders. Without the borders showing, you'll be able to see the effect of your changes more clearly.

2   Make sure the insertion point is in the table.

3   In the Table Designer, click the Ruling icon at the top of the Table Designer.

   Here is where you can define how you want rules to appear within the table. Options include how often you want column or row rules, width of outside ruling, and heading and footer ruling.

4 Change the Column Ruling options and Body Row Ruling options to None.

5 Click Update All. The ruling between the body cells is removed.

6 In the Heading And Footing Ruling area, change Separators to TableTop and Rows to None.

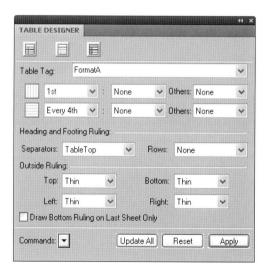

7 Click Update All. The ruling between the Project Sales row and the subsequent data is removed.

	2011	2010	2009	2008
				MODUL 9
Projected Sales:				
United States	203,461	146,992	89,557	72,429
Western Europe	157,700	90,853	55,650	47,005
Eastern Europe	101,006	72,448	35,543	30,451
Western Asia	49,349	30,557	20,512	15,627
Eastern Asia	32,544	12,953	6,430	350
Australia	12,542	9,600	5,398	3,213
South America	556,602	363,403	213,090	169,075
Canada	35,601	51,525	42,508	12,954
Philippines	20,428	10,327	6,972	3,451
Southeast Asia	3,655	2,153	1,078	446
Total assets	616,286	427,408	263,648	185,921

Saving a new table format

Now that you have edited the Format A table to your liking, you will save this as a new table format. If you decide to create a new table that is similar to this one, you simply apply that formatting via the Table Designer.

1 With your cursor inside the table, choose New Format from the Table Designer.

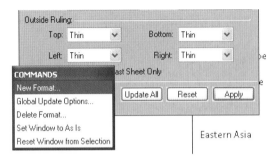

2 Name it **Modul9_table**.

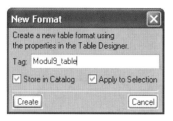

3 Click Create.

4 Save your work.

Custom ruling and shading

The table is almost finished, but you need to shade the *2010* heading to highlight the results. Because the additional shading you need doesn't follow a pattern, you can't specify it in the table format. Instead, you'll define some custom shading for the table.

1 Drag from the heading cell that contains the text *2010* to the right to select the cell.

	2011	2010	2009	2008	MODUL 9
Projected Sales:					
United States	203,461	146,992	89,557	72,429	
Western Europe	157,700	90,853	55,650	47,005	
Eastern Europe	101,006	72,448	35,543	30,451	
Western Asia	49,349	30,557	20,512	15,627	
Eastern Asia	32,544	12,953	6,430	350	
Australia	12,542	9,600	5,398	3,213	
South America	556,602	363,403	213,090	169,075	
Canada	35,601	51,525	42,508	12,954	
Philippines	20,428	10,327	6,972	3,451	
Southeast Asia	3,655	2,153	1,078	446	
Total assets	616,286	427,408	263,648	185,921	

Note: Zooming in to a higher percentage makes it easier to see slight differences in line thickness when editing ruling styles.

2 Choose Table > Custom Ruling & Shading.

3 Click Edit Ruling Style under the Apply Ruling Style area.

4 Type **Red** for the name of the new ruling style.

5 Choose Red for the color and type **2.0** for the width.

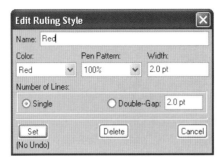

6 Click Set.

7 Choose Red from the Apply Ruling Style menu.

8 In the Custom Ruling and Shading dialog box, set the Fill to 30% and the color to Red.

9 Click Apply.

10 At the top of the table, select the four cells in the row containing the years.

11 In the Custom Ruling and Shading dialog box, set the Fill to **30%** and the color to **Red**.

12 Click Apply.

	2011	2010	2009	2008
MODUL 9				
Projected Sales:				
United States	203,461	146,992	89,557	72,429
Western Europe	157,700	90,853	55,650	47,005
Eastern Europe	101,006	72,448	35,543	30,451
Western Asia	49,349	30,557	20,512	15,627
Eastern Asia	32,544	12,953	6,430	350
Australia	12,542	9,600	5,398	3,213
South America	556,602	363,403	213,090	169,075
Canada	35,601	51,525	42,908	12,954
Philippines	20,428	10,327	6,972	3,451
Southeast Asia	3,655	2,153	1,078	446
Total assets	616,286	427,408	263,648	185,921

13 Click outside the table to see the results.

14 Save and close the file.

You have finished this lesson.

For in-depth information about tables and file formats, visit www.adobe.com/support/framemaker.

Review questions

1 What is tab-delimited text?

2 What are two ways to resize columns?

3 How do you make the contents of one cell straddle two or more cells?

4 What is the difference between the normal ruling and shading you can apply from the Table Designer and the custom ruling and shading you can apply from the Custom Ruling and Shading dialog box?

Review answers

1 In tab-delimited text, each paragraph represents a row of the table, with tabs separating the contents of one cell from another.

2 Select the columns. Then either drag a handle at the right side of the column or choose Table > Resize Columns, enter a value in the To Width text box, and click Resize.

3 To straddle cell content across multiple cells, drag from the cell containing the text, through the cells you want the text to straddle. Then choose Table > Straddle.

4 Only ruling and shading that extend through the entire table or across one or more rows or columns in a repeating pattern can be created and applied with the Table Designer; they are then part of the table format. Ruling and shading that extend only partway across a table or that span individual cells are created and applied with the Custom Ruling and Shading dialog box. Such ruling and shading are not part of the table format.

10 ADDING CROSS-REFERENCES AND FOOTNOTES

Lesson overview

In this lesson, you'll learn how to do the following:

- Insert cross-references to headings
- Insert cross-references to specific words or phrases in a paragraph
- Insert cross-references to other documents
- Insert footnotes
- Change footnote properties

 This lesson takes approximately one hour to complete. If you have not already copied the resource files for this lesson onto your hard drive from the Lesson10 folder on the *Adobe FrameMaker 9 Classroom in a Book* CD, do so now. If needed, remove the previous lesson folder from your hard disk.

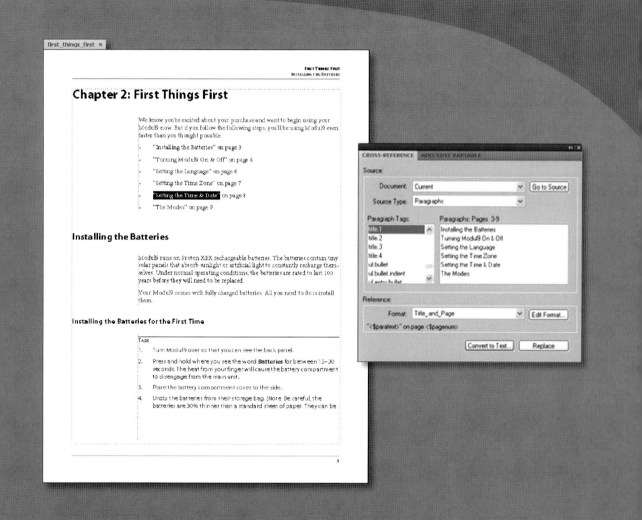

Getting started

A cross reference is an instance within a document which refers to related or synonymous information elsewhere within the document. When you need a cross-reference, in FrameMaker you simply specify the source and the wording you wish to use. Later, if page numbers or headings change when you edit the source documents, FrameMaker 9 can automatically update the cross-references. Similarly, as content shifts and edits occur, FrameMaker 9 can rearrange and renumber footnotes as you move through the production process.

In this lesson, you'll use an introductory document for Modul9 to learn and practice how to add cross-references and footnotes.

Internal cross-references

In this exercise, you'll learn about internal cross-references by editing an existing one. An internal cross-reference is one that links to the same document in which it originates. You will begin by exploring a paragraph cross-reference. A paragraph is any piece of text that ends with a hard return.

Viewing a paragraph cross-reference

Note: Cross-references are typically —but not necessarily— attached to heading text. (Remember that a heading is still, technically, a paragraph.)

1 Choose File > Open, and select first_things_first.fm in the Lesson10 folder.

2 Click Open.

3 Click once on the text in the first bulleted item ("Installing the Batteries"). Notice the entire line selects automatically.

4 Double-click on the text to open the Cross-Reference panel.

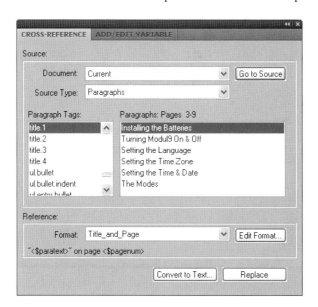

This cross-reference is set to refer to a heading within the current document. The reader is pointed to that paragraph to learn more about installing the Modul9's batteries.

5 Click on the next three bulleted items to see they are all set up as cross-references.

The last two bulleted items are not yet set up as cross-references. You will do this next.

Inserting a cross-reference

You'll now start to insert a cross-reference to a heading. This is called a *paragraph cross-reference* because the reference is applied to an entire paragraph.

1 Triple-click to entirely select the fifth bulleted item, "Setting the Time & Date."

> **Note:** A paragraph is any amount of text that ends with a paragraph symbol. This means that even a one-line heading is a paragraph, and has a paragraph format associated with it.

2 In the Cross-Reference panel, you specify the paragraph you want to refer to (the *source* for the cross-reference) and the wording you want to use (the cross-reference format).

You'll refer to a heading.

3 If necessary, select title.1 from the Paragraph Tags list. The text of all title.1 paragraphs appears in the Paragraph list to the right.

4 Choose Setting The Time & Date from the Paragraphs list.

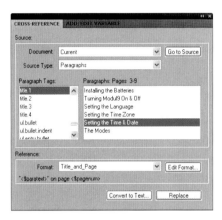

Next, you'll use the Format menu in the Reference area to specify the format for the cross-reference. The name of the format appears in the menu, and the definition appears below.

5 If necessary, choose Title_and_Page from the Format menu. This format definition includes the text of the heading and the page number on which it occurs.

6 Click Replace. The type you selected gets replaced with the same text. Because you selected the entire paragraph (including the End of Paragraph symbol) previously, press Enter to reinsert a break between the fifth and sixth bullets.

7 Save the document.

8 Click once on the new cross-reference (the text that FrameMaker 9 just inserted). Notice that the entire cross-reference is selected, indicating that FrameMaker 9 considers it a single object, not a series of words.

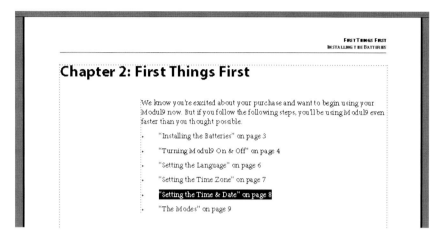

● **Note:** You can't edit the text of the cross-reference directly. The text is tied to the source, and will automatically update when opening files and updating books. If you want to refresh the information displayed in a cross-reference, use the Edit > Update References... menu item. However, you can change it by choosing a different cross-reference format, by referring to a different heading, or by editing the definition of the format.

Now you'll repeat the process for the final bulleted item.

9 Click and drag to select the text for the last bulleted item.

10 If the Cross-Reference panel is still open, proceed to Step 11. If not, right-click on the selected text, and choose Cross-Reference.

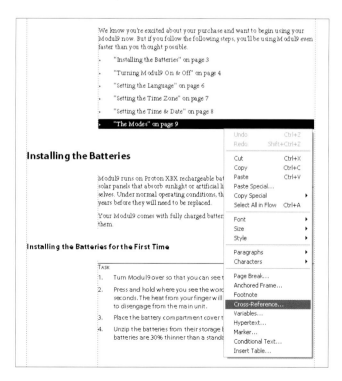

11 Choose title.1 from the Paragraph Tags list.

12 Ensure that The Modes is chosen in the Paragraphs list, and Title_and_Page is chosen in the Format menu.

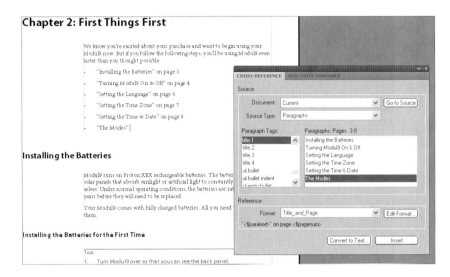

13 Click Replace.

Displaying the source of a cross-reference

You can use the cross-reference to go to the source paragraph quickly.

1 Since your reference to The Modes is still selected, click the Go To Source button in the upper right of the Cross Reference panel. FrameMaker 9 jumps to the source heading on page 9 (7 of 8).

2 Choose View > Text Symbols (if they are not already on) to display the marker symbol (⊥) that appears at the beginning of the heading. The marker defines the location of the cross-reference source.

The marker symbol is difficult to see because it's at the beginning of the paragraph. You can confirm that it's there by zooming to 400%.

3 Click the arrow to the right of the current zoom percentage in the status bar, and choose 400%.

4 Reset your zoom to 100%.

External cross-references

The cross-reference you inserted in the previous exercise referred to a heading in the same document. Now you'll insert an external cross-reference, that is, a cross-reference to a heading in a different document. You can create an external cross-reference to any other FrameMaker document, but in order to do so, both the source and the destination files must be open on the same computer.

Add troubleshooting.fm to your workspace

1 Choose File > Open, and select troubleshooting.fm from the Lesson10 folder.

2 Drag to arrange the two documents, first_things_first.fm and troubleshooting. fm, so that you can see at least part of both of them.

Note: If the documents are appearing in tabbed view, simply drag the tabs of each document to separate them from the tabbing. Then you will be able to see both documents easily.

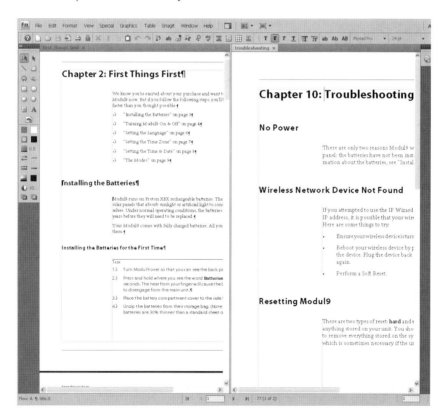

3 On the second page of first_things_first.fm (which is labeled page 4), click at the end of the last paragraph on the page.

Turning Modul9 On & Off¶

When Modul9 is in its cube configuration, you will see a power button on the top panel. You will use this power button to both turn the Modul9 on and off.¶

4 Press the spacebar, type **For information on resetting Modul9, see**, and press the spacebar again.

> ## Modul9 On & Off¶
>
> When Modul9 is in its cube configuration, you will see a power button on the top panel. You will use this power button to both turn the Modul9 on and off. For information on resetting Modul9, see¶

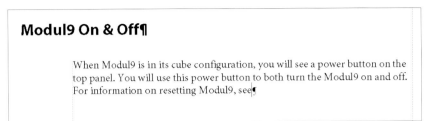

5 If the Cross Reference panel is not already open, right-click and choose Cross-Reference.

6 Choose troubleshooting.fm from the Document menu at the top of the dialog box.

7 Verify that title.1 is still selected in the Paragraph Tags list.

8 Select Resetting Modul9 in the Paragraphs list.

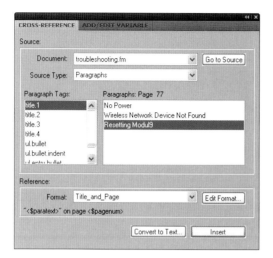

9 Click Insert. The cross-reference appears at the insertion point.

> When Modul9 is in its cube configuration, you will see a power button on the top panel. You will use this power button to both turn the Modul9 on and off. For information on resetting Modul9, see "Resetting Modul9" on page 77¶

10 Type a period.

In first_things_first.fm, the cross-reference to the title.1 in troubleshooting.fm has been made.

11 Save both documents.

Now that the cross-reference is inserted and saved, FrameMaker 9 will update its text and page number automatically whenever you print or open the file, or update a book, or you can manually update the file.

Footnotes

FrameMaker 9 makes it easy to add footnotes to documents. It also automatically rearranges and renumbers footnotes as needed, as you edit your documents.

Inserting footnotes

You'll start off by adding add a brief footnote to the text.

1 Go to the first page of first_things_first.fm.

2 Choose View > Text Symbols to turn on text symbols, if necessary.

3 Under the "Installing the Batteries for the First Time" heading, click at the end of step 2.

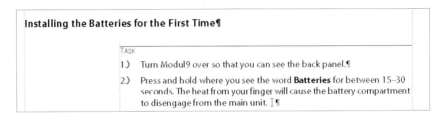

4 Choose Special > Footnote. A footnote reference number now appears where you clicked, and an empty footnote appears at the bottom of the page with a separator line between it and the body text, with a blinking text insertion point.

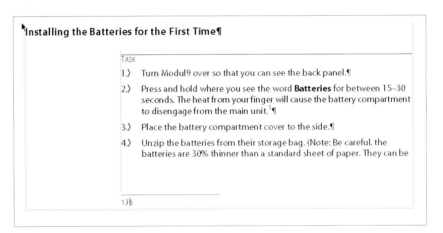

5 Type **The average battery life for Modul9 is 7-10 years. Replacement batteries can be ordered online**.

6 Save the document by pressing Ctrl+S.

Changing how footnotes look

Footnote properties come from two sources. First, because footnotes are paragraphs of text, a normal paragraph format controls a footnote's indents, font, and so on. Second, to handle a footnote's unique aspects (such as its numbering style), there is a special Footnote Properties dialog box. In this section, you'll make changes to properties from both sources.

Removing the separator line

You'll remove the line that separates the body of the text from the footnotes. The separator is specified on a special *reference page*, so you'll change it there. (A reference page is a nonprinting page containing graphic frames.) The contents of the graphic frames can be used by paragraph formats and footnotes.

1 If necessary, choose View > Borders to turn on borders.

2 Choose View > Reference Pages.

The reference page contains several reference frames. The fourth one contains the footnote separator line.

3 Click the line inside the footnote frame to select the line (not the frame). You may want to zoom in to 200% to make it easier to click the line inside the frame.

4 Press Delete to remove the line, leaving just the empty Footnote frame. Even without the line, the frame defines the space between the body text and the first footnote in the column.

Note: When you insert the first footnote in a column, FrameMaker 9 uses the Footnote reference frame to determine how much space to leave between the body text and the footnote. If the reference frame contains a line, FrameMaker 9 displays that line within the space.

5 Choose View > Body Pages to redisplay page 2. The separator line is now gone, but the space is still there.

1.} The average battery life for Modul9 is 7-10 years. Replacement batteries can be ordered online.§

Changing footmote pagination

In the sample document you've been working with, each footnote appears at the bottom of the column that contains the footnote reference. By changing the paragraph format for the footnote, you'll make the footnotes span all columns and sideheads.

1 Click in the footnote at the bottom of page 1. Note that the status line's tag area displays Footnote. This is the tag of the format you'll change.

2 Choose Window > Panels > Paragraph Designer.

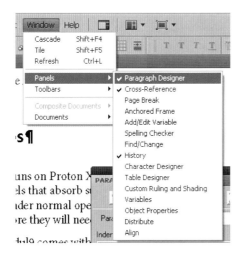

3 Click the Pagination icon at the top of the Paragraph Designer.

4 In the Format area, select Across All Columns And Side Heads. This will allow the footnotes to span across the page.

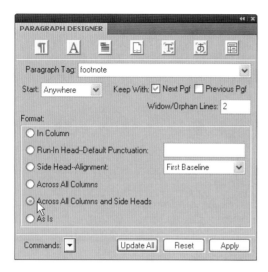

5 Click Update All. The footnote now spans the page.

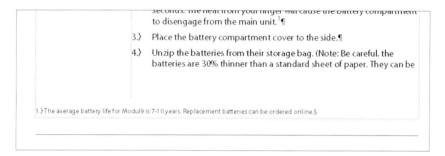

6 Close the Paragraph Designer.

7 Save and close first_things_first.fm.

Review questions

1 What is a paragraph cross-reference?

2 How can you quickly display the source of a cross-reference?

3 What controls the wording and appearance of a cross-reference?

4 After you've typed the text of a footnote, how can you return to the spot you left off in the body text?

5 What controls the look of a footnote?

Review answers

1 A paragraph cross-reference refers to the text of an entire paragraph. Inserting a paragraph cross-reference places a marker at the source automatically.

2 To quickly display the source of a cross-reference, double-click the cross-reference, and then click Go To Source.

3 The cross-reference format, which is chosen in the Cross-Reference dialog box, determines the wording and appearance of a cross-reference. You create and edit the cross-reference format by clicking Edit Format in that dialog box.

4 Choose Special > Footnote again to return the insertion point to the body text.

5 The look of a footnote is determined by the settings in the Footnote Properties dialog box and by the paragraph format specified for footnotes.

11 GENERATING BOOKS

Lesson overview

In this lesson, you'll learn how to do the following:

- Create a book file
- Add documents to a book and paginate them
- Add a table of contents to a book
- Format a table of contents

 This lesson takes approximately one hour to complete. If you have not already copied the resource files for this lesson onto your hard drive from the Lesson11 folder on the *Adobe FrameMaker 9 Classroom in a Book* CD, do so now. If needed, remove the previous lesson folder from your hard disk.

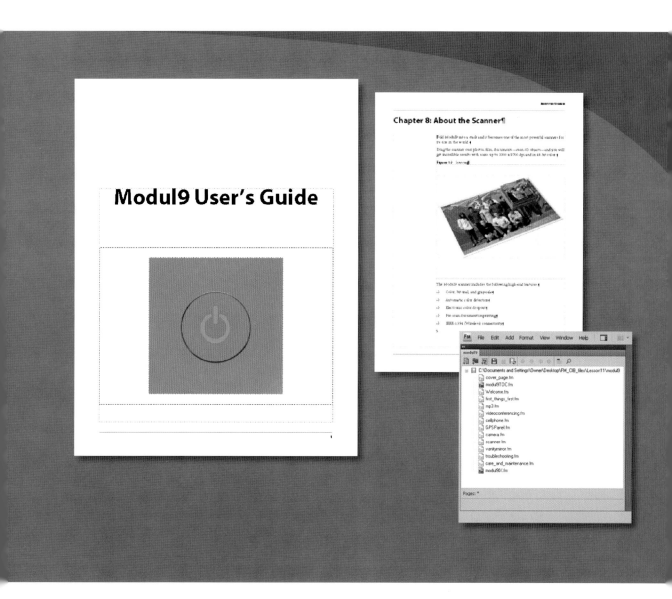

Getting started

You can group separate FrameMaker 9 documents into one book. This grouping—a *book file*—lets you associate and work with several documents together, and makes it easy to paginate across files, update things like cross-references, and generate special documents such as a table of contents or index for the entire book. It also greatly simplifies updating and formatting. (For more information on building indexes within FrameMaker 9, see Chapter 12.)

This lesson uses five sample files. You'll collect these files into a book and then generate a table of contents from all the files in the book.

You'll create a directory for Modul9 using all the files in this lesson.

1   Open modul9.book in the Finished folder of the Lesson11 folder.

The Book panel opens, and displays a list of all the files contained within it.

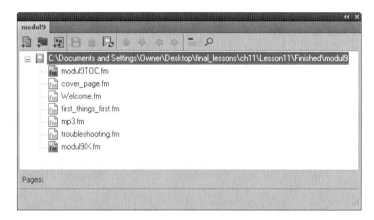

2   Click on the name of the first file, and then Shift-click on the last file to select all the files in the book.

3 Right-click, and choose Open from the context menu.

⬤ **Note:** Pressing the Shift key while choosing the File menu will allow you to choose Open All Files In Book.

All the files open and appear in tabbed view in the work area.

⬤ **Note:** To "activate" a document in the window, click its tab at the top of the window to show it.

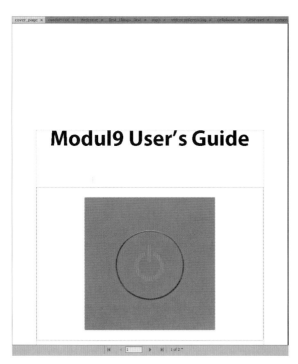

4 Click on the name of the first file in the Book panel, and then Shift-click on the last file to select all the files in the book.

5 Right-click, and then choose Close from the context menu. Because you are working in the Book panel, you will be closing all the currently selected files.

Next, you will open a file from the lesson files and use it as the base file for a new book. You will open cover_page.fm.

1 Select File > Open and navigate to the main Lesson11 folder.

2 Choose cover_page.fm and click Open.

3 Be sure to open it from the main Lesson11 folder. You'll be using it in the next exercise. You won't be making copies of the sample files in this lesson. If you want to start over, you can get fresh copies of the files from the CD.

Book file basics

In this exercise, you'll explore working in a book window and compare it to working in a document window. First you'll create a new book file.

Creating a book file

1   Choose File > New > Book.

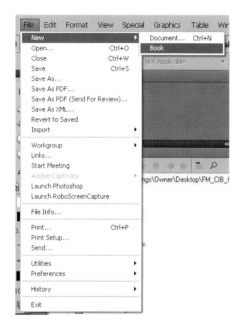

2   Click Yes when FrameMaker 9 displays an alert message asking if you want to add cover_page.fm to the new book.

3   Click Yes.

Note: Because you have a file open, FrameMaker prompts you to add coverpage. fm to the new book.

Note: When you're working in a book window, the menu bar contains only commands appropriate for books. For example, the File menus for a book and for a document contain somewhat different commands.

A book window appears showing the book's contents—which so far is only cover_page.fm (the file from which the book was created).

Main file menu when a book is the active file.

Main file menu when a document is the active file.

For the rest of this lesson, you'll work with the book rather than with individual files in the book. So you'll close the actual document, but leave open the book window you just created.

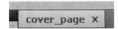

1   Click the X on the tab next to cover_page.fm at the top of the document to close it.

2   If prompted to save changes, click No.

The book was assigned a default name (UntitledBook1.book), but you'll save the book using a more appropriate filename.

3 Click the Save icon ( ) at the top of the Book panel, enter the filename **modul9_guide**, be sure that the destination folder is Lesson11, and click Save. (FrameMaker will add the .book extension to the filename, since it is a book file.)

● **Note:** The Save Book command saves the book file only. The component files of the book are saved individually. If you save the book to a new location, open and save each individual component file to that location as well.

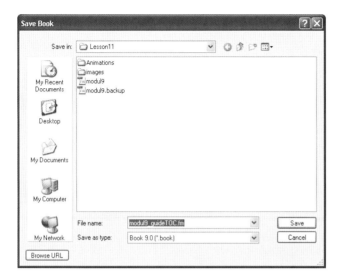

An alternative way to get to the same dialog box is to choose File > Save Book, enter the filename **modul9_guide**, be sure that the destination folder is Lesson11, and click Save.

Adding documents to the book

Your book will eventually contain a table of contents and five chapters. You'll add another chapter now.

1 Click the Add Files icon ( )at the top of the Book panel.

2 Navigate to the folder containing the chapter files, select first_things_first.fm, and click Add.

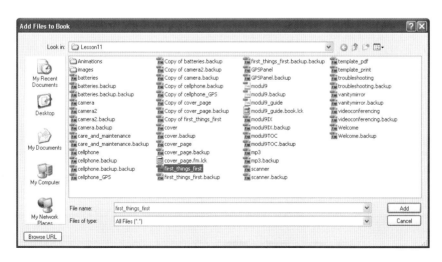

FrameMaker adds the file to the book, but doesn't open it.

Next, you will add another file and reorder the files within the Book panel.

3   Choose Add > Files, choose Welcome.fm, and then click Add.

Welcome.fm is now added at the bottom of the list of book files. It needs to be moved to just after the cover_page.fm document.

4   Select Welcome.fm in the book window and click the up arrow on the book panel to move the file to just below cover_page.fm.

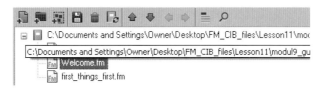

5   Add the remaining book files: first_things_first, mp3, troubleshooting and Welcome.

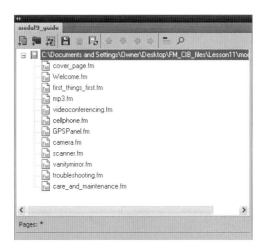

6   Rearrange one or more files in a book window, if necessary, by selecting them and dragging them where you want them to appear in the book.

7   Choose File > Save Book to save the book file.

Opening files from the book window

Before adding a table of contents to the book, you'll take a quick look at the individual chapters in the book.

1   Double-click welcome.fm in the book window.

Double-clicking a filename is a quick way to open an individual file. However, you can open many files at once by using shortcuts.

2   In the book window, hold down Shift and choose File > Open All Files In Book. All the documents in the book are opened.

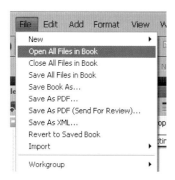

● **Note:** Hold down Shift and choose File > Close All Files In Book to close the preface and all four chapters. Leave the book window open.

Table of contents

The book is now complete except for the table of contents. This will be a *generated file*—a file whose entries are generated from the other files in the book.

Adding a table of contents is a two-step process. First, you define the table of contents in the book file. Then you create (generate/update) the table of contents from the other files in the book.

Adding a table of contents

1   In the book window, select a file close to the top of the list of book file—in this case, Welcome.fm—because you want the book's table of contents to appear above Welcome.fm.

2   Choose Add > Table Of Contents.

In the Set Up Table Of Contents dialog box that appears, you'll choose chapter titles and one level of headings to be included in the table of contents.

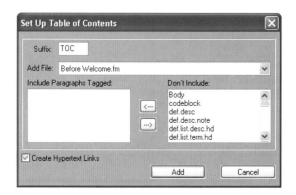

▶ **Tip:** If you place the TOC in a different place, you can always move it later and update the book to correct the entries.

Initially, the tags of all the paragraph formats in the files of the book appear in the Don't Include list on the right. When you set up a table of contents, you decide which tags to include in it. FrameMaker 9 will look in the files of the book for any text that's formatted with these tags. When it finds a paragraph formatted with one of the tags, FrameMaker 9 copies the text into the table of contents.

You'll include the paragraph tagged title.0 in the table of contents by moving it from the right (the Don't Include list) to the left (the Include Paragraphs Tagged list).

Tip: If you have a long Don't Include list, and especially if you know the names of your paragraph tags, you can type the first few letters of the format name, and the list will jump down to that entry.

3 Select title.0 in the right scroll list (you may need to scroll down) and move it to the left scroll list by clicking the left arrow in the middle of the dialog box ⌊<⋯⌋ —not the left arrow on your keyboard.

Moving title.0 to the Include Paragraphs Tagged list means that the text of any paragraph tagged title.0 will be included in the book's table of contents. In this sample book, each chapter contains a single paragraph tagged title.0.

4 Double-click title.1 in the Don't Include list to move it to the Include Paragraphs Tagged list. (Double-clicking an item in either of these lists moves the entry to the opposite list.)

The text of any paragraph tagged title.1 will also be included in the table of contents. Each chapter contains several paragraphs tagged title.1.

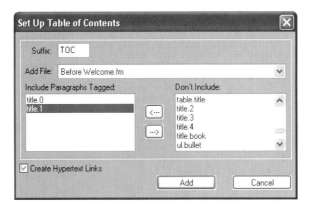

5 Click Add.

You will work with the dialog box that appears—the Update Book dialog box—in the next exercise.

Generating the table of contents

In the Update Book dialog box that appears, the filename of the table of contents, modul9_guideTOC.fm, appears in the Generate list. The filename is based on the book's name, with, obviously, TOC (table of contents) appended.

The modul9_guideTOC.fm file itself doesn't actually exist until FrameMaker 9 *generates* it—meaning that FrameMaker 9 gathers the paragraphs tagged with the formats you want included (title.0 and title.1), and puts them into a new file called modul9_guideTOC.fm.

Note: If you had placed a document in the book folder that was already named modul9_guideTOC.fm, FrameMaker 9 would have used that document for the table of contents instead of creating a new one. If that document contained definitions for the TOC formats, FrameMaker 9 would have used that document for the table of contents instead of creating a new one. This is one of the ways you can use a template to speed up formatting a generated file.

1   In the Update Book dialog box, deselect Apply Master Pages, if necessary.

2   Click Update to generate the table of contents for your book.

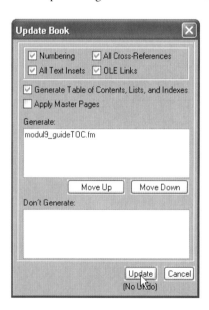

Note: You can generate the TOC without opening all files in a book. However, if the chapter files require user intervention to resolve problems with missing fonts, graphics, or other resources, the TOC will not update properly. If this happens, hold down the Shift key and choose File > Open All Files In Book. After resolving any missing resource issues, proceed to update the book, using the Update Book icon at the top of the Book panel.

During the update process, if you've applied the settings as described here, FrameMaker 9 updates the chapter numbering, page numbering, and cross-references in the book as well as the TOC.

Messages appear briefly in the status bar at the bottom of the book window as FrameMaker 9 examines each file in the book. If the TOC does not open automatically after processing, open it now by double-clicking on it in the book window. Initially, the table of contents uses the default page layout of the first document in the book (the preface).

3 Open the table of contents.

4 Click in the first paragraph (line) of the table of contents; notice the tag that appears in the status bar: title.0TOC.

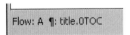

5 Press the Down Arrow key several times to move the insertion point down the page, noticing that the other paragraphs also have tags that end in "TOC" (title.1TOC).

Flow: A ¶: title.1TOC

FrameMaker 9 created and assigned these TOC paragraph formats when the table of contents was generated. Because these formats are initially identical, the entries in the table of contents all look the same. Later, you'll redefine the formats and apply them to the entries in the table of contents.

6 Choose File > Save.

Pagination and numbering

The table of contents shows you how FrameMaker 9 has paginated the book. You'll notice that many of the chapters and page numbers still start with "1." That is because FrameMaker does not number chapters, pages, or paragraphs consecutively across documents in a book file unless you tell it to.

Now you'll learn how to make sure that the chapters are numbered correctly, and then the pages.

Setting up page numbering

1 Double-click first_things_first.fm in the book window to open the document. Notice that the page numbers still start with 1.

2 Return to the book window, select mp3.fm, and then Shift-click to select all files up to and including care_and_maintenance.fm.

3 Choose Format > Document > Numbering.

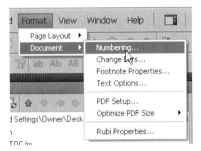

4 Choose Chapter from the pop-up menu, select Continue Numbering From Previous File In Book, and click Set.

5 Choose Edit > Update Book, and then click Update.

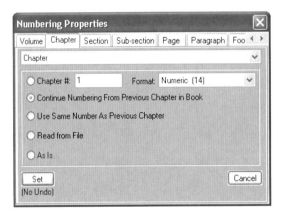

6 If prompted to continue, click OK.

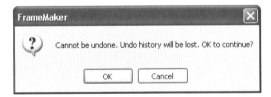

Fixing the pagination

You've already learned how to use Format > Document > Numbering; now, you'll learn a different command—a *context menu*—for adjusting subsequent pagination.

Note: A context menu contains commonly used commands that are applicable to the item under the pointer when you invoke it—a very convenient shortcut when working in a book window.

1 Make sure the book file is open and visible.

2 Select first_things_first.fm, and then Shift-click care_and_maintenance to select all subsequent chapters in the book.

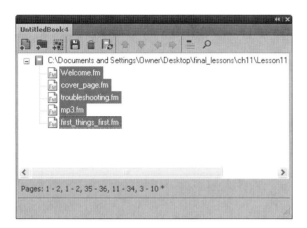

3 Right-click, and choose Numbering from the context menu.

4 Click the Page tab at the top of the Numbering Properties dialog box.

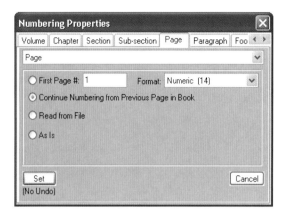

5 Click Continue Numbering From Previous Page In Book.

6 Click Set.

7 Click OK to respond to the "cannot be undone…OK to continue" message.

8 Choose Edit > Update Book, and then click Update.

9 Reopen the table of contents to see the new numbering. Notice that the book's pages are now numbered sequentially.

⬤ **Note:** Any time you make a change to a file in a book—either to its contents or to its setup—you should update the book to see the change reflected in the book's generated files.

Making book format changes

Once the book is created, you may wish to make changes to certain aspects, such as the layout, and other formatting. You will now explore ways to edit the book's formatting. You will begin by changing the layout of the book.

Changing the TOC layout

The chapters in the book use a side-head area at the left side of each page. To make the TOC consistent with the rest of the book, you'll apply the same layout, and add roman numbering to the pages. The roman numbering will help set this section apart from the remainder of the book.

First convert the TOC's own page number to roman.

1 With the TOC document still open, choose Format > Document > Numbering.

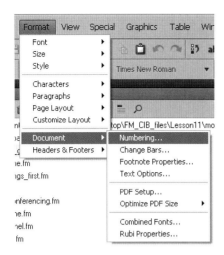

2 Click the Page tab at the top of the Numbering Properties dialog box.

3 In the First Page # text box, type **1** if it isn't already there.

4 In the Format pop-up menu, choose Roman (xiv), and click Set. Observe the number at the bottom-right corner of the table of contents document. It is now set in roman numerals.

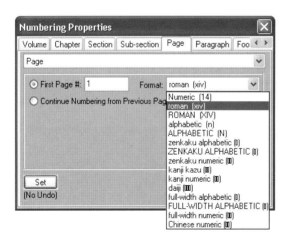

Next, you'll format the page layout of the text contents of the TOC itself.

5 Go to View > Options and affirm the units you are working with are points.

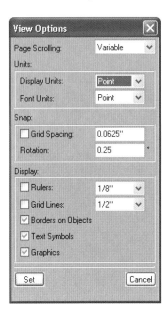

Click anywhere in the table of contents, and then choose Format > Customize Layout > Customize Text Frame.

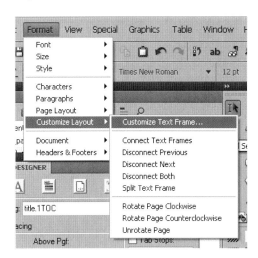

6 Select Room For Side Heads. Change the Width to 92. Verify that the Gap is 14 and the Side is set to Left.

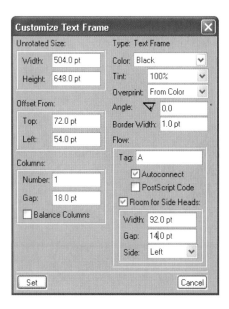

7 Click Set. The entries move into the body-text area at the right side of the text frame.

Adding a title

Before you format the entries in the table of contents, you'll create a custom color for use when you add a title.

You will begin by defining the color you wish to use in the document's title.

1 Choose View > Color > Definitions.

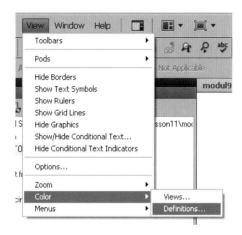

2 From the Color Libraries menu, choose Pantone Uncoated.

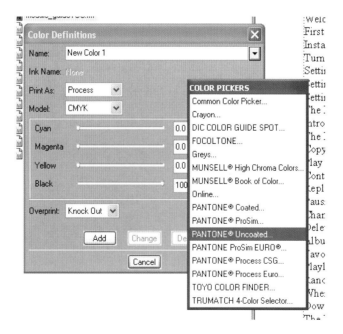

3 Type **292** in the Find field, and click Done.

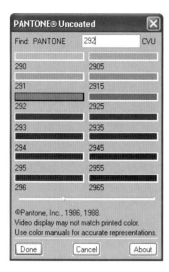

4 In the next dialog box, click Add, and then click Done.

Now you will use the newly defined color in your TOC heading format.

5 Place your cursor at the beginning of the first paragraph of the table of contents.

6 Press Enter to create a new paragraph at the top, and then press the Up Arrow key to place the insertion point in that new empty paragraph.

7 Type **Table of Contents**.

8 Make the Paragraph Designer the active panel.

9 Choose New Format from the Commands menu at the bottom of the Paragraph Designer.

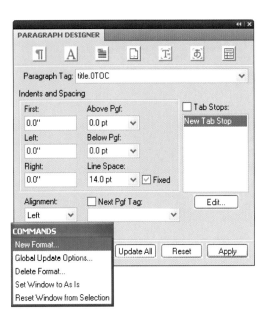

10 Enter **title.contents** in the Tag text box. Make sure that both options—Store In Catalog and Apply To Selection—are selected.

11 Click Create.

The tag of the title you just typed is changed to **title.contents** (as shown in the status bar), and the format is stored in the Paragraph Catalog.

When you generate the table of contents again, FrameMaker 9 will update only the paragraphs whose tags end in *TOC*. The TOC title will remain as is, because the tag you typed (**title.contents**) doesn't end in *TOC*.

12 In the Paragraph Designer, click the Default Font icon at the top of the window.

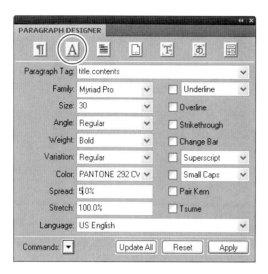

13 Change the Family to Myriad Pro, the Size to 30, the Weight to Bold, the Color to Pantone 292, and the Spread to 5.

14 Click Update All to change the title and to update the format in the catalog.

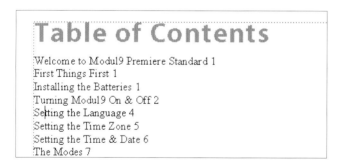

Formatting TOC entries

When formatting a table of contents you will:

- make changes that affect the contents of the entries, instead of their formats.

- format the entries as you would any paragraphs.

Formatting a generated file takes some time, but once you are happy with it FrameMaker 9 reuses your formatting each time you generate the file. You can also use the formatted table of contents from one book as a template for others, so the investment you make in formatting things correctly can pay off quickly.

Changing the contents of entries

The table of contents now has the general appearance you want, but the entries still may not be quite right for the intended design. For example, suppose you'd like the preface and chapter titles to appear without page numbers. Also, all the Heading1 entries now need to contain tab characters to complete the formatting process.

Changes such as these affect the contents of entries rather than their formats. For this reason, you won't be using the Paragraph Designer to make the changes. Instead, FrameMaker 9 provides a special place to edit the contents of TOC entries: a *reference page*.

1   Choose View > Reference Pages.

You need to locate the page containing your TOC definition.

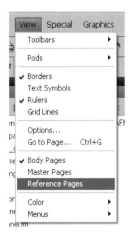

2 Click the Next Page button in the status bar until you reach the TOC Reference page (on page 4). The name of the reference page appears in the status bar.

Note: The Find command (Ctrl+F) will allow you to choose TOC from the list of available reference pages.

The page contains text that controls the contents of the entries in the table of contents. The first paragraph—which is just one line long and whose text is <$paratext> <$pagenum>—is tagged title.1TOC.

This paragraph contains two *building blocks*, <$paratext> and <$pagenum>. Building blocks are special pieces of text that control the content of an entry. In this case, <$paratext> and <$pagenum> indicate that the text of the preface title and its page number should appear in the table of contents. The space between the two building blocks tells FrameMaker 9 to insert a space between the text and the page number.

3 Highlight the <$pagenum> at the end of the line with the title1.TOC paragraph tag applied to it. Delete the <$pagenum> building block and the space before it. This instructs FrameMaker 9 to place only the text of the preface title in the table of contents.

4 Press the Down Arrow key until the insertion point is in the last paragraph (tagged title.0TOC). The paragraph tag appears in the status bar.

5 Place the insertion point at the end of the paragraph and press Backspace to delete the <$pagenum> building block and the space before it. This instructs FrameMaker 9 to place only the text of each chapter title in the table of contents.

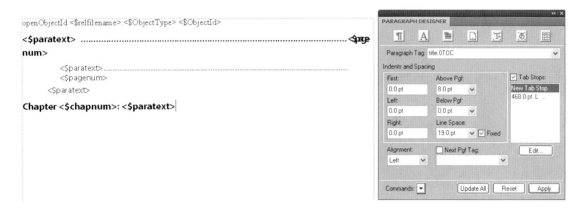

6 Press the Up Arrow key to place the insertion point in the second paragraph (tagged **title.1TOC**).

7 Select the space between the two building blocks and press Tab to replace the space with a tab character.

The special text flow on the TOC reference page now looks like this.

¶
<$paratext> ¶
<$paratext>⟩<$pagenum>¶

§

8 Choose View > Body Pages.

Your recent changes are not reflected in the table of contents until you generate the table of contents again.

9 Save the table of contents, and keep it open.

10 Return to the book window, and choose Edit > Update Book.

11 Click Update.

⬤ **Note:** If you get an Inconsistent Numbering dialog box, select the Skip Remaining Inconsistent Numbering Properties Messages checkbox to proceed. Then go to your book file, hold the Shift key and choose File > Save All Files in Book.

12 Review the updated table of contents and notice that page numbers no longer appear next to the preface or chapter titles, and that all the title1.TOC page numbers are now right-aligned with leader dots.

13 Save the table of contents by choosing File > Save.

Changing paragraph formats

1 Click in the first entry (Welcome to Modul9) in the Modul9_guideTOC.fm file.

2 In the Paragraph Designer, display the Default Font properties.

3 Change the Family to Myriad Pro, the Size to 12, and the Weight to Regular.

4 Click Update All.

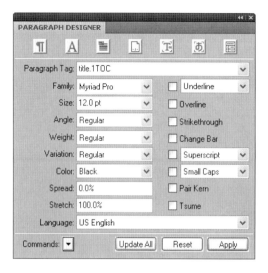

5 Click in the third entry (Installing the Batteries).

6 In the Paragraph Designer, change the Family to Myriad Pro.

7 Click Update All.

8 Save the document.

Adding tab leader dots

A table of contents often places page numbers at the right side of the page with dots between the text and the page numbers.

To do this for all entries, you need to make a few more changes to the format of the entries.

1 Choose View > Rulers to display the document rulers.

2 If the Paragraph Formatting toolbar isn't visible, choose View > Toolbars > Paragraph Formatting.

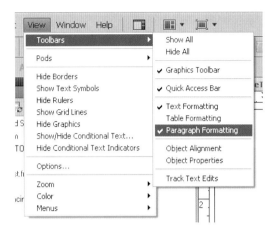

The formatting bar contains several formatting icons you can use to set some paragraph properties. You'll use the tab stops.

3 Click anywhere in the Installing the Batteries entry. Note that this is a title.1TOC paragraph.

4 Click the Right Tab icon (⬇).

5 Click on the top ruler, just under the right indent on the ruler, to add a tab.

Only the Installing the Batteries entry receives the right aligned tab you just created. You'll update the rest of the entries in a while.

6 Double-click the tab stop (the little arrow) under the ruler.

7 In the Edit Tab Stop dialog box that appears, select the second dotted leader in the Leader area.

8 Click Edit.

9 If you are prompted with another dialog box, click OK.

10 In the Paragraph Designer, click Update All. Each title.1TOC entry now uses a right aligned tab with a dot leader to display its page number.

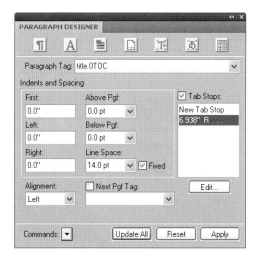

11 Close the Paragraph Designer.

12 Choose View > Rulers to hide the rulers, and then save the document.

You've completed this lesson. For in-depth information about books, tables of contents, and other generated lists such as lists of figures and lists of tables, visit *Adobe FrameMaker 9 Help*.

Review questions

1 What are some of the advantages of using a book file?

2 Where do you find the commands you need for working with a book file?

3 How do you access a context menu for a book window?

4 When you set up a table of contents for a book, why do you have to move some tags to the Include Paragraphs Tagged list?

Review answers

1 A book file creates and keeps current a bookwide table of contents or index. It also simplifies chapter and page numbering and helps to maintain accurate cross-references.

2 Commands that apply to a book file appear in the File, Edit, and Add menus when a book window is active. Also, you can access a book window's context menu for a subset of the commands.

3 To display a context menu, right-click in the book window.

4 Moving tags in the Set Up Table Of Contents dialog box tells FrameMaker 9 which paragraphs to include when it creates and updates the table of contents.

12 CREATING INDEXES

Lesson overview

In this lesson, you'll learn how to do the following:

- Add an index to a book

- Generate and update an index

- Lay out an index

- Apply formatting to an index

- Insert and edit index entries

 This lesson takes approximately one hour to complete. If you have not already copied the resource files for this lesson onto your hard drive from the Lesson12 folder on the *Adobe FrameMaker 9 Classroom in a Book* CD, do so now. If needed, remove the previous lesson folder from your hard disk.

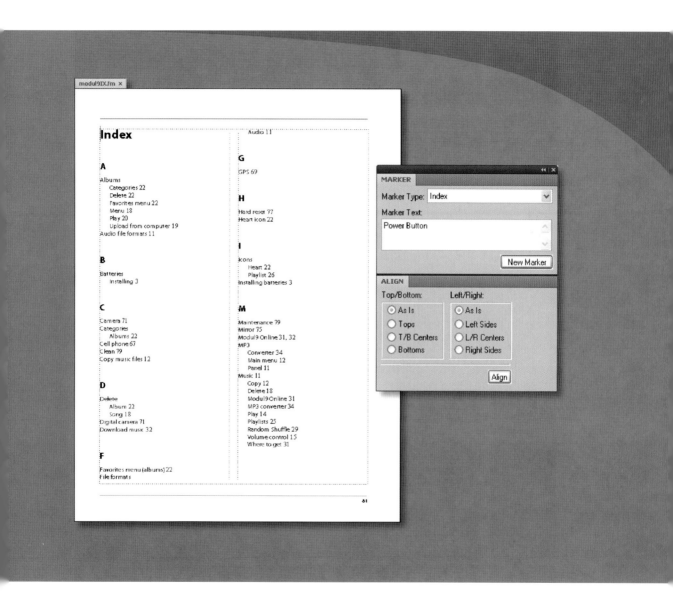

You prepare an index by inserting special markers.
After the markers are inserted, you can generate an
index for a document or for an entire book. When you
move or edit a marker, you generate the index file
again so that it's up to date.

Getting started

This lesson uses a version of the book file you created in the previous lesson. This version will contain four sample files: a preface file, a TOC, and three chapter files (first_things_first.fm, mp3.fm, videoconferencing.fm, and troubleshooting.fm). These files are already collected into a *book file*—a file that lets you group and work with several documents together—for a small guide to Modul9, and a table of contents was generated from all the files in the book. As you saw in Lesson 11, book files let you easily paginate across files, update all cross-references, and generate special documents such as an index or table of contents for the book.

You won't be saving copies of the sample files in this lesson. If you want to start over, you can get fresh copies of the files from the CD.

Adding an index to a book

Adding an index to a book takes a few steps. First you add a description of the index to the book file; then you generate the index from index markers that are already inserted in the book's chapters. (Later in this lesson, you'll insert and edit some index entries on your own.)

1 Open modul9.book in the Lesson12 folder.

2 Select troubleshooting.fm in the book file (because you'll want the index to follow the last chapter in the book).

3 Choose Add > Standard Index.

The dialog box that appears is already set up for a standard index.

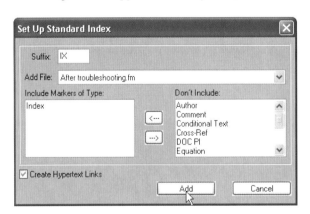

4 Make sure that Create Hypertext Links is selected so that FrameMaker 9 will include a hypertext link with each index entry. You'll use this feature later

to display the source of an index entry by Ctrl+Alt-clicking the entry's page number in the generated index.

5 Click Add.

The index filename—modul9IX.fm—appears in the Update Book dialog box. The filename is based on the book's name (*IX* is the default suffix for a book's first standard index). The modul9IX. fm *file* doesn't actually exist until FrameMaker generates it (meaning that FrameMaker gathers and sorts the index markers into the index file).

6 Click Update.

Messages appear briefly in the status bar at the bottom of the book window as FrameMaker scans each file in the book. If the index were already open, FrameMaker would finish the update by

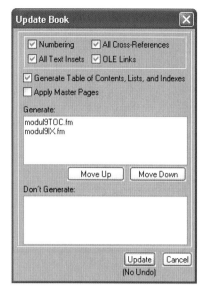

making it the active file. It's not open (you just created it) so double-click your new index in the book file to open it now.

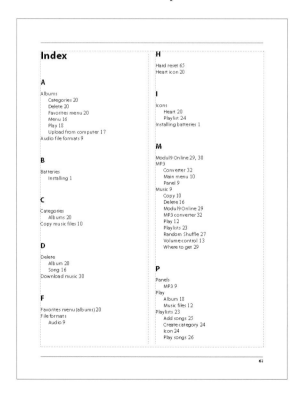

Note: If the program fails to generate the index, make sure the book file is active, hold down the Shift key, choose File > Open All Files In Book, and resolve any missing resource messages that appear. Then proceed to generate the index, using the steps described above.

Note: The index has content because the chapters already contain index markers. If you hadn't yet inserted any index markers, the index would be empty. You'll add more index markers yourself later.

Formatting the index

Initially, the index uses the page layout of the first document in the book (in this case, first_things_first.fm). If you had a template for the index, you could have generated a formatted index, and you'd be finished now. However, there is no template for this index, so you'll need to format it yourself.

If you don't already have a template, you'll probably want to add some formatting. When you regenerate an index, it will retain the formatting changes. What's more, you can use the formatted index as a template for other indexes.

The first change you'll make to the appearance of the index are to its layout. You'll change to a three-column layout.

Changing the page layout

1   In the index file, choose View > Master Pages to display the Right master page.

2   Click in the main text frame, and choose Format > Customize Layout > Customize Text Frame.

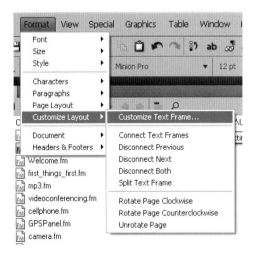

3   In the Columns area, change the number of columns to **3**, and select Balance Columns.

When columns are balanced, text on the last page of the index is evenly distributed across the columns.

4 Ensure that Room For Side Heads is deselected, and then click Set.

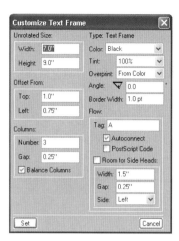

5 In the status bar, click the Previous Page icon (◀) to display the Left master page.

6 Click in the main text frame, and choose Format > Customize Layout > Customize Text Frame.

7 Make the same changes you made for the Right master page (three balanced columns, no side heads), and then click Set.

8 Choose View > Body Pages to display the first page of the index.

The layout changes throughout the index.

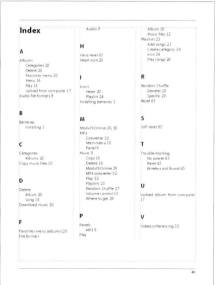

9 Save your work.

Formatting main entries

Now you'll format the main entries (the ones tagged Level1IX in the status bar).

1   Click in the first index entry ("Albums").

2   In the Paragraph Designer, display the Default Font properties.

3   If necessary, change the Family to Myriad Pro, the Size to 10, and then click Update All.

All the main entries are reformatted.

4   Display the Pagination properties.

5   Change the Widow/Orphan Lines setting to 3. This setting controls the minimum number of lines that can appear alone at the top or bottom of a column. A setting of 3 will prevent multiline entries from splitting across columns or pages.

6   Click Update All.

7   Display the Advanced properties.

Hyphenate has a check next to it, indicating hyphenation is turned on.

8 Click the box until it is blank to turn it off, and then click Update All.

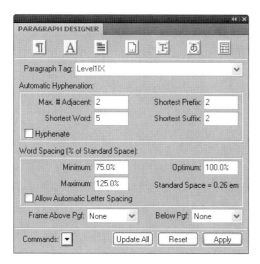

The main (Level1IX) entries are formatted.

Formatting subentries

Now you'll format the subentries (the ones tagged Level2IX).

1 Click in the first subentry under Albums ("Categories").

2 With the Advanced properties displayed in the Paragraph Designer, click Hyphenate twice to turn it off.

3 Click Update All.

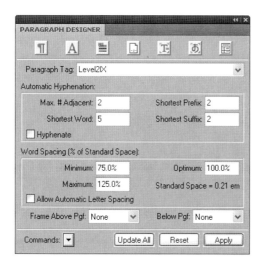

4   Display the Pagination properties, and change the Widow/Orphan Lines setting to **3.**

5   Check the box next to Previous Pgf, in the Keep With section. This will ensure any Level 2 entries remain with the Level 1 entries, in the event of a break.

6   Click Update All.

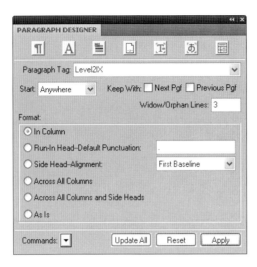

7   Display the Default Font properties.

8   If necessary, change the Family to Myriad Pro, the Size to 10, and the Spread to 5, and then click Update All.

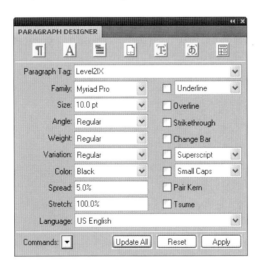

9   Display the Basic properties.

10 If necessary, change the Alignment to Left and the Left indent to .75, and then click Update All.

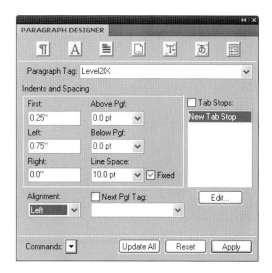

The subentries (Level2IX entries) are formatted.

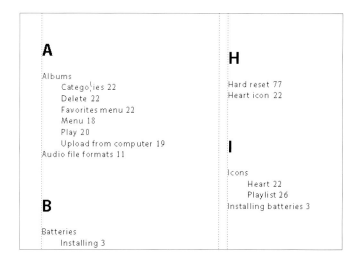

Formatting group titles

Finally, you'll format the group titles (the paragraphs containing the letters *A, B, C*, and so on). Group titles are tagged GroupTitlesIX.

1 Click in the first group title (the letter *A* in the first line under the title).

2 With the Basic properties displayed in the Paragraph Designer, change the Space Above Pgf to **14 pt**, and click Update All.

3 Display the Default Font properties, and change the Family to Myriad Pro, the Size to **12**, the Weight to Bold, and the Color to Dark Grey. Then click Update All.

4 Under the Pagination properties, choose Across All Columns from the Format section.

The group titles are formatted.

A
Albums
    Categories 20
    Delete 20
    Favorites menu 20
    Menu 16
    Play 18
    Upload from computer 17
Audio file formats 9

B

Batteries
    Installing 1

C

5 Save the index.

Adding and editing index entries

An index entry is contained in a *marker* that you insert in the source text. Index entries are accessible via a panel, so you can go back and edit, remove, or amend them at any time.

Adding primary and secondary index entries

You'll add a main entry and a subentry to the index.

1 In the book window, double-click first_things_first.fm to open the file.

2 If necessary, choose View > Text Symbols to display text symbols.

3 In the chapter's status bar, click the Next Page button (▶) to display the second page of the chapter.

4 Click just to the left of the first instance of the words "power button" in the last paragraph on the page.

5 Choose Special > Marker.

6 If necessary, move the Marker panel so it doesn't obscure your view of the insertion point in the chapter.

7 In the Marker panel, make sure Index is chosen in the Marker Type menu.

8 Click in the Marker Text box, and enter **Power Button**.

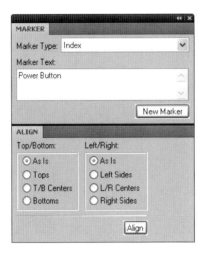

9 Click New Marker to insert the index marker. A marker symbol (**T**) appears at the insertion point. The next time you generate the index, an entry will appear for "Power Button."

10 Save and close first_things_first.fm.

11 From the book window, click the Update Book button.

12 Click Update in the Update Book dialog box to generate the index.

After a few moments, the index is updated.

13 Notice the new entry for "Power Button" appears on the first page in the third column.

Editing index entries

After you generate an index, you may want to go back and make changes simply based on now having seen the index in its entirety, or you may have found errors in the index. For example, in this sample index, there are two entries for the power button, and one is not capitalized. You will delete the second entry, so there will be one entry with two page numbers.

1 Place your text cursor over the "powers button" entry.

2 Ctrl+Alt-click on the page number.

The cursor changes to a pointing finger.

3 Click the entry.

First_things_first.fm appears, with the index marker selected.

4 Choose Special > Marker.

5 Delete the "s" at the end of the word "powers."

6 Capitalize "Power Button."

7 Click Edit Marker.

8 Save the file.

9 In the book window, click the Update Book icon.

10 In the Update Book dialog box, click Update.

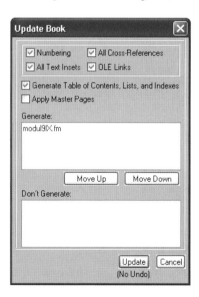

11 In the modul9IX file, check the Power Button entry, and verify there is one listing referring to two page numbers.

12 Save your work.

Review questions

1   When you first add an index to a book file, does FrameMaker 9 automatically create that file on disk?

2   How are the paragraph formats Level1IX and Level2IX created and used?

3   How do you go to the source of an index marker from within the index file?

Review answers

1   No. Adding an index to a book file only sets up some of the properties for the index file, such as its pagination and what markers will be used to compile it. You must use the Update Book dialog box to actually generate (create) the index file for the first time.

2   FrameMaker 9 automatically creates and assigns these formats to the main index entries (Level1IX) and to subentries (Level2IX). By modifying the properties of these formats, you can quickly format the text of the index entries.

3   To view the source file for an index marker in the index file, position the cursor in the index entry, and then hold down Ctrl+Alt while you click the page number.

13 CONDITIONAL TEXT

Lesson overview

In this lesson, you'll learn how to do the following:

- Apply condition tags to text

- Create condition tags and assign condition indicators

- View different versions of a conditional document

- Save versions of conditional documents

 This lesson takes approximately one hour to complete. If you have not already copied the resource files for this lesson onto your hard drive from the Lesson13 folder on the *Adobe FrameMaker 9 Classroom in a Book* CD, do so now. If needed, remove the previous lesson folder from your hard disk.

Chapter 2: First Things First¶

We know you're excited about your purchase and want to begin using your Modul9 Ultra Premiere now. But if follow the following steps, you'll be using Modul9 Ultra Premiere even faster than you thought possible.¶

- •) "Installing the Batteries" on page 3¶
- •) "Turning Modul9 Ultra Standard Premiere On & Off" on page 4¶
- •) "Setting the Language" on page 6¶
- •) "Setting the Time Zone" on page 7¶
- •) "Setting the Time & Date" on page 8¶
- •) "The Modes" on page 9¶

Installing the Batteries¶

Modul9 Ultra Premiere runs on Proton XBX rechargeable batteries. The batteries contain tiny solar panels that absorb sunlight or artificial light to constantly recharge themselves. Under normal operating conditions, the batteries are rated to last 100 years before they will need to be replaced.¶

Your Modul9 Ultra Premiere comes with fully charged batteries. All you need to do is install them.¶

Installing the Batteries for the First Time¶

Task
1.) Turn Modul9 Ultra Premiere over so that you can see the back panel.¶
2.) Press and hold where you see the word **Batteries** for between 15–30 seconds. The heat from your finger will cause the battery compartment to disengage from the main unit.¶
3.) Place the battery compartment cover to the side.¶
4.) Unzip the batteries from their storage bag. (Note: Be careful, the batteries are 30% thinner than a standard sheet of paper. They can be

3

If you're preparing several versions of a document, each with minor differences, you can use a single FrameMaker 9 file for all the versions. When you later revise the contents, you'll be revising all the versions at the same time. The one file can contain all versions using conditional text and conditional graphics.

Viewing conditional text

Conditional text is a powerful feature of FrameMaker, used for creating multiple versions of the same document. For example, a teacher's version of a handout or textbook would contain margin notes and other extras not included in the student version. Catalogs with different regional pricing or health benefits brochures for full- and part-time employees are also good examples of documents that would benefit from the use of conditional text.

This lesson's sample is a document depicting features of the Modul9 Standard. You'll use conditional text to add information about a second and third model: the Modul9 Premiere and the Modul9 Ultra. When you're finished, the three versions will be contained in one document.

The user of the document will have the option to show the text for any of the three models, all from within a single document.

Before you add information about the Modul9 Premiere, you'll take a look at the finished document.

1 Open finished.fm in the Lesson13 folder.

Note: Finished.fm already contains information about two models of Modul9: Standard and Premiere.

2 If they are not already visible, show borders and text symbols by choosing those commands from the View menu.

3 Choose Special > Conditional Text > Conditional Text.

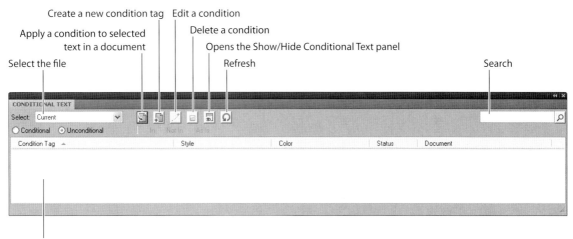

Create a new condition tag   Edit a condition

Apply a condition to selected   Delete a condition
text in a document

                  Opens the Show/Hide Conditional Text panel

Select the file   Refresh   Search

List of condition tags and their attributes

4 Click the Show/Hide icon to open the Show/Hide Conditional Text panel.

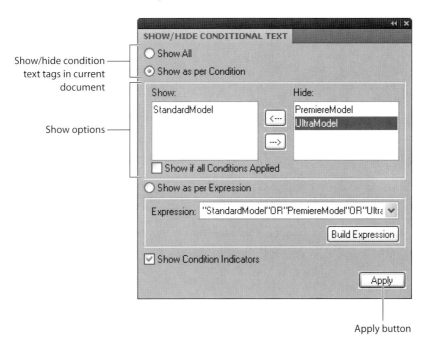

Show/hide condition text tags in current document

Show options

Apply button

The StandardModel tag is set to show, and the PremiereModel tag is set to hide.

5 Double-click the StandardModel tag to move it to the Hide window, and double-click the PremiereModel tag to move it to the Show window.

6 Click Apply.

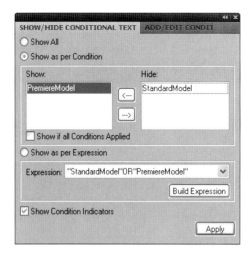

Notice the Premiere text is now showing on the document, and the Standard text is hidden.

🌐 **Note:** Condition indicators (in this example, the blue underlining) are present so that you can easily identify what text is in which condition. You have the option of choosing different colors and indicators such as underline or strikethrough, to easily see the differences between versions. When the document is ready for final printing, you would turn these indicators off.

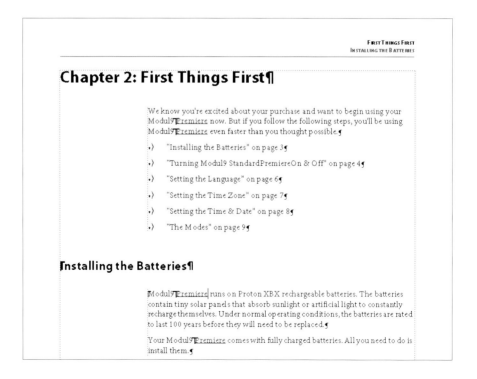

7 Close finished.fm without saving changes. Close the Show/Hide Conditional Text panel, but leave the Conditional Text dialog box open; you'll use it often during this lesson.

Next, you'll add another condition text tag, for the Ultra Model.

Adding and managing conditional text

The document you'll be working with contains only the information for the standard and premiere models. You will add the conditional information on the Ultra model.

Setting up the document

When working with conditional text, it is beneficial to have your text symbols and borders showing.

1 Open three_models.fm in the Lesson13 folder.

2 Choose File > Save As, enter the filename **three_models1.fm**, and click Save.

3 If borders and text symbols are not turned on, choose View > Borders and then choose View > Text Symbols.

You're ready to begin working with conditional text.

Creating condition tags

First you'll create the condition tags that will indicate the new version of this document.

1 If the Conditional Text pod isn't open, choose Special > Conditional Text > Conditional Text.

● **Note:** When working with conditional text, it is often helpful to have borders and text symbols showing. Seeing symbols such as paragraph breaks and markers can be useful when determining conditional text.

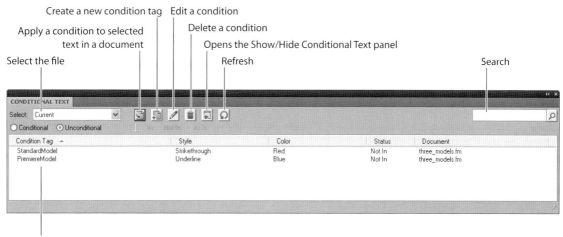

Create a new condition tag   Edit a condition
Apply a condition to selected text in a document   Delete a condition
Opens the Show/Hide Conditional Text panel
Select the file   Refresh   Search

List of condition tags and their attributes

You will set up the condition for the Ultra model first. No text needs to be selected at this time.

2 Click the Create New Condition Tag icon ( ). The Add/Edit Condition Tag panel appears.

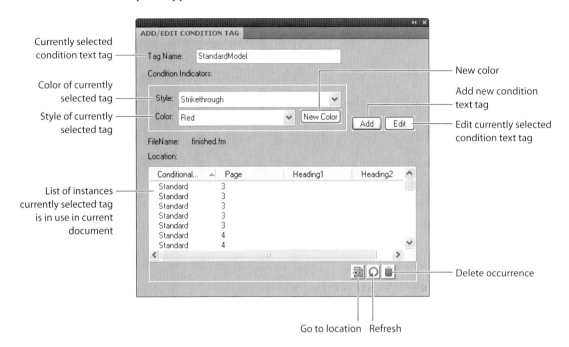

Currently selected condition text tag

Color of currently selected tag

Style of currently selected tag

List of instances currently selected tag is in use in current document

New color

Add new condition text tag

Edit currently selected condition text tag

Delete occurrence

Go to location   Refresh

3 Replace the contents of the Tag Name text field with **UltraModel**.

4 Choose Overline from the Style menu and Green from the Color menu.

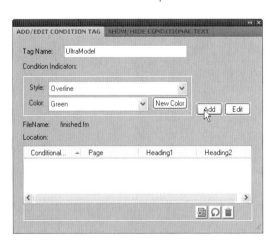

5 Click Add. The new condition tag appears in the Conditional Text panel.

6 Save the document.

You have added a new condition tag by editing an existing one. Next, you'll apply the new tag to text in your document.

Adding conditional text

In this exercise, you'll add conditional text for the Ultra model, and then temporarily hide the Premiere tags.

1 On the first page of the document, place the insertion point at the end of the first instance of the word Premiere, in the first paragraph.

> We know you're excited about your purchase and want to begin using your Modul9 Premiere now. But if you follow the following steps, you'll be using Modul9 Premiere even faster than you thought possible.
>
> •} "Installing the Batteries" on page 3
>
> •} "Turning Modul9 StandardPremiereOn & Off" on page 4

2 Type **Ultra**.

As you type, the new text picks up the existing condition text tag, but you will fix that.

3 Click and drag to select the word Ultra.

4 In the Conditional Text dialog box, click the radio button next to Conditional, and then click the radio button next to In.

5 Choose Ultra from the tag list.

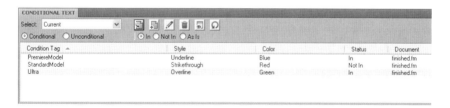

6 Click the Apply ( ) icon.

> We know you're excited about your purchase and want to begin using your Modul9 Premiere Ultra now. But if you follow the following steps, you'll be using Modul9 Premiere even faster than you thought possible.

The selected text appears in the UltraModel style, but because it was previously tagged with Premiere, it has the characteristics of the PremiereModel tag as well, so you will need to remove the Premiere tag from the text.

7 With the word Ultra still selected, click the Not In radio button from the Conditional Text panel, and click the PremiereModel tag.

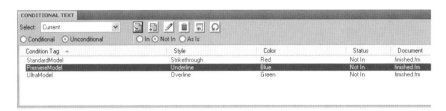

8 Click the Apply icon to remove the PremiereModel characteristics from the word Ultra in your document.

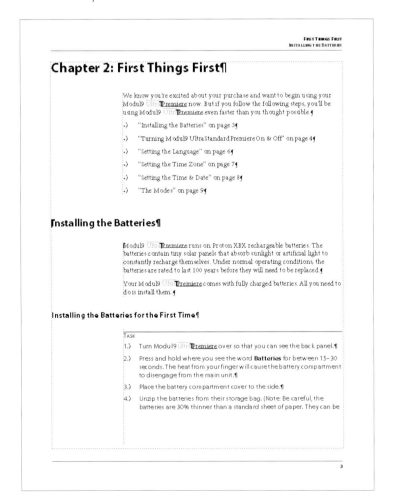

Tagging text as you type

If you work extensively with conditional text, you may find it easier and more efficient to use keyboard shortcuts to apply and remove condition tags. In this exercise, you'll use keyboard shortcuts to add conditional text to the body paragraph, this time using the UltraModel condition tag.

1 Navigate to page 7 (5 of 8) of the document.

2 Click to place the insertion point at the end of the first paragraph, ending with Preferences panel.

3 Type a space, and then type **Modul9Ultra has the capability of adding up to 150 languages, available for additional purchase.**.

> There are two ways you can set the language: through the initial setup or via the Preferences panel. During the steps below, you will be guided through setting the language via the Preferences panel. Modul9Ultra has the capability of adding up to 150 languages, available for additional purchase.

4 Select the sentence you just typed.

> There are two ways you can set the language: through the initial setup or via the Preferences panel. During the steps below, you will be guided through setting the language via the Preferences panel. Modul9Ultra has the capability of adding up to 150 languages for additional purchase.

5 Press Ctrl+4. A menu appears in the status bar to prompt you for a condi-tion tag.

6 Type the letter **U**. Because the UltraModel condition tag is the only one that begins with the letter U, the menu is able to directly select that tag.

> ✓ Not Applicable
>
> PremiereModel
> StandardModel
> UltraModel

> There are two ways you can set the language: through the initial setup or via the Preferences panel. During the steps below, you will be guided through setting the language via the Preferences panel. Modul9Ultra has the capability of adding up to 150 languages, available for additional purchase.

7 Save the document.

▶ **Tip:** If there are conditional text settings in another FrameMaker document you wish to use, you can import them via File > Import > Formats.

Saving versions of conditional documents

You'll produce a Standard version of the document. Only the StandardModel conditional text will appear, but the other text and conditions will still be stored in the document.

While FrameMaker does give you the option to delete condition text tags, it is advisable to hide the ones not in use, rather than delete them. Delete a condition tag only when you are confident you will not be using it in the future.

1 In the Conditional Text dialog box, click the Show/Hide Conditional Text icon.

2 Choose to show only the StandardModel tag, and hide the PremiereModel and UltraModel tags, double-clicking on each tag as needed.

3 Click Apply.

● Note: Conditional text can be especially useful in the Adobe Technical Communications Suite workflow, of which FrameMaker is a component. Since RoboHelp supports condition tags and maintains the conditional text setting applied, you can use these FrameMaker conditions to help you produce multiple versions of topic-based Help systems.

4 Choose File > Save As PDF.

5 Click Save.

In the PDF Setup box, choose Smallest File Size for online viewing only.

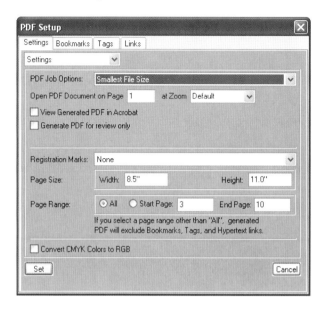

For Open PDF Document on Page, type 1.

Click Set.

6 Save and close standard.fm.

For in-depth information about conditional text, see Adobe FrameMaker 9 Help.

Review questions

1 What are the advantages of a conditional document?

2 Why is it useful to work with condition indicators showing?

3 How can you tell if text is conditional?

Review answers

1 A conditional document lets you work in a single source file but with different versions of the same document. This reduces redundancy and improves efficiency.

2 Condition indicators make it easy to see what text is in which condition. This reduces the chances of errors when editing.

3 If text is conditional, the status bar displays the condition tag for the selected text or the location of the insertion point.

14 WORKING WITH HYPERTEXT AND PDF

Lesson overview

In this lesson, you'll learn how to do the following:

- Include hypertext links in a table of contents and an index

- Modify a cross-reference format to indicate hypertext links

- Test hypertext links

- Save a book file in Portable Document Format (PDF)

This lesson takes approximately one hour to complete. If you have not already copied the resource files for this lesson onto your hard drive from the Lesson14 folder on the *Adobe FrameMaker 9 Classroom in a Book* CD, do so now. If needed, remove the previous lesson folder from your hard disk.

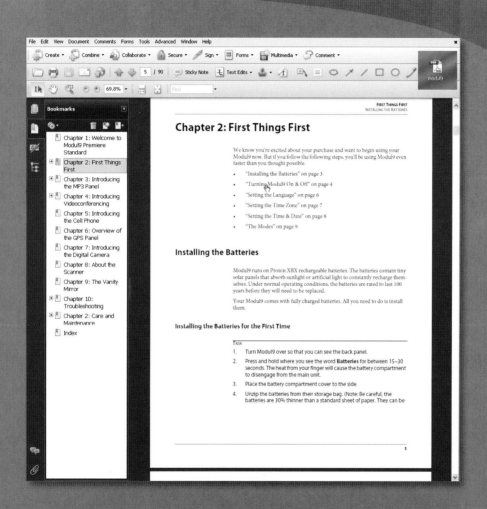

Hypertext documents make it easy to access information in a nonlinear way. (A hypertext link is a connection to another page or another document. When you click the link, it takes you to that spot automatically.) FrameMaker 9 includes a robust set of hypertext commands that can turn a document into an interactive experience.

Creating a hypertext TOC and index

Note: To see completed versions of the sample files for this chapter, open the Finished folder in the Lesson14 folder. You won't be saving copies of the sample files in this lesson. If you want to start over, you can get fresh copies of the files from the CD.

This lesson uses a book file that contains multiple chapters of the user's manual for the fictional Modul9. You'll generate a table of contents and index with automatic hyperlinks to the content. You'll then see how cross-references automatically contain hyperlinks, and you'll modify a cross-reference. Finally, you'll convert the files to Portable Document Format (PDF) to compare this type of online distribution with FrameMaker 9's built-in ability to create view-only hypertext documents (HTML).

You may recall that you've created automatic hypertext links in previous chapters when inserting cross-references, and when creating TOCs and Indexes.

Including links in a TOC and index

Modul9.book already has a table of contents and an index set up for you. You have only to make a small adjustment to the setup of these files to create hypertext links automatically.

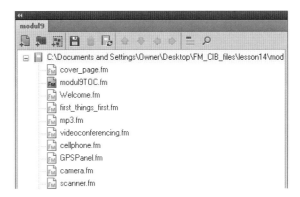

1 In the Lesson14 folder, open modul9.book.

2 Right-click on the Modul9TOC.fm file and choose Set Up Table of Contents from the context menu.

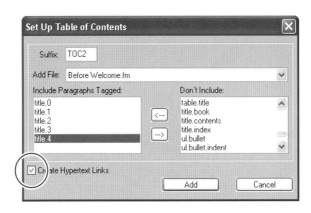

3 Verify that Create Hypertext Links is checked, and then click Set.

4 You won't generate the table of contents yet, so click Cancel to close the Update Book dialog box that appears.

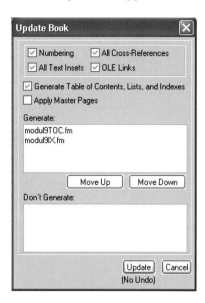

The settings will be preserved, even though you chose to not generate the TOC at this time.

Now you'll set up the index to contain hypertext links.

5 Right-click on Modul9IX.fm and choose Set Up Standard Index from the context menu.

6 Verify that Create Hypertext Links is checked, and then click Add.

Note: You can change the settings and choose to update the book later. The edited settings will be preserved, and applied when you do update the book at a later time.

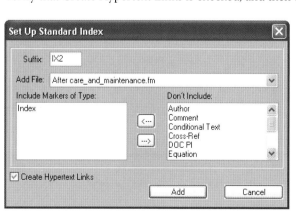

Now you'll generate the table of contents and the index from the Update Book dialog box.

7 Be sure the two files (modul9TOC2.fm and modul9IX.fm) are in the Generate list.

8 Deselect Apply Master Pages, and click Update.

⬤ **Note:** If FrameMaker produces a Book Error log, or otherwise fails to update the book, make the book file active, hold down the Shift key and choose File > Open All Files In Book. Address any dialog boxes you are presented with. The Book Error Log can assist in identifying and correcting missing resource errors. Then proceed to update the book. This doesn't necessarily correct any missing resource problems, but will allow you to update the book successfully.

Using a hypertext TOC and index

Each TOC index entry is linked to its source. In the final document, clicking the entry opens the page that contains the reference.

1 Double-click modul9TOC.fm in the book window to open the table of contents.

2 Locate the section on the first page called "Installing the Batteries," and Ctrl+Alt-click the entry to activate the hypertext link embedded in the TOC entry.

3 FrameMaker 9 opens first_things_first.fm and jumps to the section heading that contains the hypertext marker ("Installing the Batteries").

Note: Depending the current setting for text symbols, you will either highlight the heading or its hypertext marker.

If you wish, go back to the TOC and repeat the previous step on another entry.

4 Double-click the index file in the book window.

Tip: Index entries often have multiple page references. To activate a hypertext link in an index, you usually Ctrl+Alt-click a page number instead of the text of the index entry.

5 Test the hypertext links. Ctrl+Alt-click the entry, with the cursor on the page number.

6 When you're finished, close all the documents, but keep the book window open.

7 Save the book file.

Note: In the final PDF and HTML documents, the user will single-click the link to go to the reference.

Testing a cross-reference link

Every cross-reference you insert in a document can be used as a hypertext link to its source. FrameMaker automatically inserts hypertext links when you insert cross-references.

We've created a cross-reference that you can use to test a hypertext link.

1   Double-click first_things_first.fm in the book window to open the first chapter file, if it isn't already open.

2   In the bulleted list on page 1, find the cross-reference item "Setting the Time & Date."

3   Ctrl+Alt-click the cross-reference to activate the hypertext link.

4   FrameMaker 9 jumps to the source of this cross-reference entry—in this case, to the start of the section on setting the time and date. Note: Notice the marker is selected. Be careful not to delete the marker as that would result in an Unresolved Cross Reference.

Formatting a hypertext cross-reference

When you are creating a hypertext application for online use, it's helpful to draw attention to objects that are links. This is especially true for cross-references, which usually look like regular paragraph text.

1   In the document first_things_first.fm, go to the first page and in the bulleted list at the top of the page, double-click the cross-reference "The Modes." This opens the Cross Reference panel.

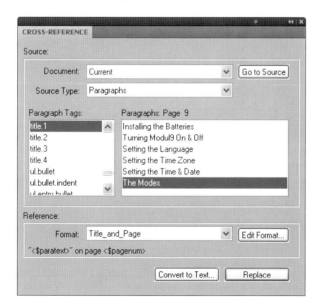

You'll change the format for this so it stands out as a hypertext link.

2 Click Edit Format. The Edit Cross-Reference Format dialog box appears.

The format for this cross-reference is called Title_and_Page, and its definition is "<$paratext>" on page <$pagenum>.

You'll now modify this format to use a character format that will make the text blue and underlined, so that it's clear that a cross-reference is a hypertext link.

1 Click at the start of the definition to place the insertion point.

2 Scroll to the end of the Building Blocks list to find the character format building block named <link.hyper>, then click it. The definition now includes <link.asis> and looks like this:

<link.hyper> "<$paratext>" on page <$pagenum>

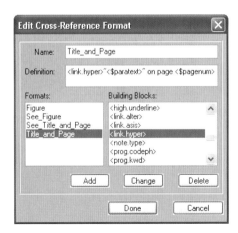

The <link.hyper> format will make the text blue and underlined so users can easily spot the hypertext links.

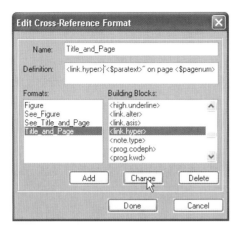

3 Click Change, then Done. The Update Cross-References dialog appears.

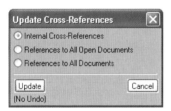

4 Make sure Internal Cross-References is selected, then click Update.

All the cross-references in the document that use the Title_and_Page format change to blue and underlined.

5 Save and close the document.

Saving as HTML

To convert a FrameMaker document to HTML, save it as an HTML file. Saving as HTML sets up definitions for how each FrameMaker format converts, or maps, to an HTML element. You can save a whole book as HTML.

FrameMaker automatically creates the mappings of formats to HTML elements upon initial conversion to HTML, but you can fine-tune them.

1 Open any document in the book.

2 Choose File > Save As HTML.

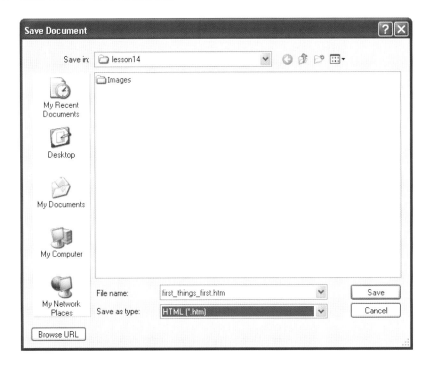

It is a good idea to choose a separate directory for the files created by a conversion to HTML, since you might create a number of them. Keeping the files in a separate directory also makes it possible to move them without changing their relative relationships.

3 Give the filename an extension of .htm, specify the file location, and click Save.

The converted file is saved where you specified.

4 Open the HTML file in a Web browser to review the converted file.

Saving as PDF

In FrameMaker 9, you can save a document or a book directly as a Portable Document Format (PDF) file. Readers can use the free Adobe Reader to view PDF files. PDF files can also be viewed in most Web browser windows.

Bookmarks can be created automatically when saving as PDF. Bookmarks are a set of interactive text links that appear in the Bookmarks panel inside the PDF document.

Saving as PDF preserves the design and format of the original and creates a compact, online system with many automatic hypertext features enabled. For example, cross-references or any hypertext links in FrameMaker 9 may become links in the PDF file.

1 If it isn't still open, open the modul9.book file.

2 Choose File > Save As PDF, and navigate to the folder where you want to save the PDF file.

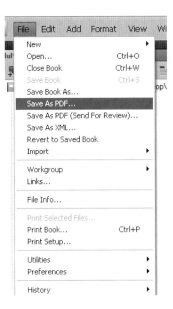

3 Enter **modul9.pdf** as the filename, and click Save.

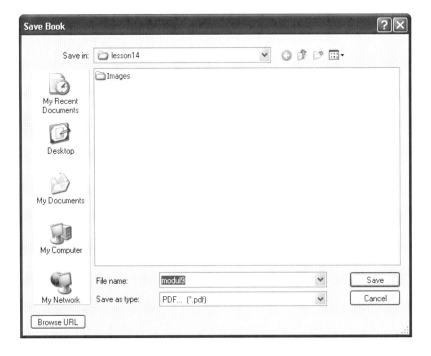

The PDF Setup For Selected Files dialog box appears.

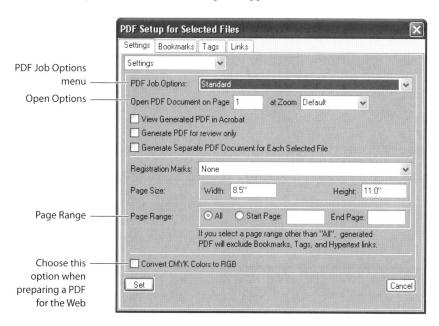

PDF Job Options menu —

Open Options —

Page Range —

Choose this option when preparing a PDF for the Web —

4 Click the Bookmarks tab at the top of the window.

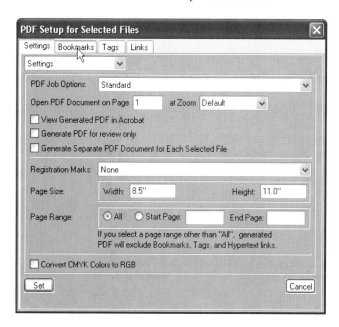

Here, you'll specify what paragraph styles you want to appear as Acrobat "bookmarks" in the final PDF file—title.0, title.1, title.2, and title.index.

5 If necessary, double-click on any paragraph style listed above to add it to the Include Paragraphs column. Double-click on any extra paragraph tags to move back to the Don't Include column.

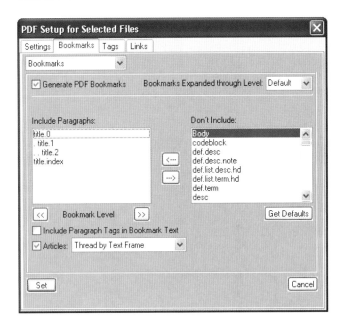

Note: Anyone who has Acrobat or Adobe Reader installed can view the PDF file.

6 Click Set. After a few moments, the modul9.pdf file appears in the folder you specified.

7 Open Adobe Reader (or Acrobat) and open the modul9.pdf file, or just double-click the modul9.pdf file if you have either of those applications on your computer.

Because you generated the table of contents and the index with hypertext links, those links are active in the PDF file as well.

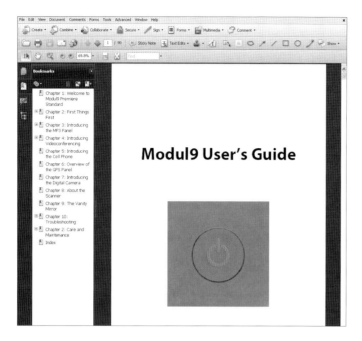

8 Click on Chapter 2: First Things First in the Bookmarks navigation pane to move to that section.

9 Click Turning Modul9 On & Off in the bulleted list at the top of the page.

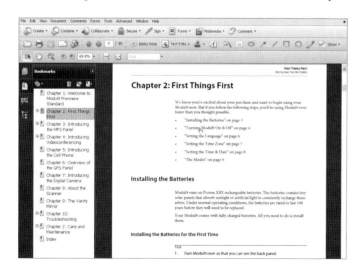

The cross-reference in the PDF takes you to that section.

10 When you're finished exploring, quit Acrobat or Adobe Reader, and close all open files in FrameMaker 9.

For in-depth information about hypertext, see Adobe FrameMaker Help.

Review questions

1 How can you automatically create hypertext links for an index?

2 What other type of hypertext link does FrameMaker 9 automatically create?

3 How can you test a hypertext link when the document is still editable?

4 How do you specify Acrobat bookmarks when you save as PDF?

Review answers

1 To create hyperlinks automatically when you create an index, select the Create Hypertext Links option in the Set Up Standard Index dialog box.

2 Any cross-reference or TOC links you insert into a document automatically become hypertext links in a view-only document.

3 You can use a special keystroke (Ctrl+Alt-click) to activate any hypertext command in an editable document.

4 Whatever paragraph formats you include in the Bookmarks / Include Paragraphs section in the PDF Setup For Selected Files dialog box become Acrobat bookmarks. The indentations of the paragraph formats in the scroll box determine how the bookmarks are nested in Acrobat.

INDEX

(number sign), using with page numbers, 50

* (asterisk), appearance in status bar, 50

" (quotation marks), using Smart Quotes with, 22

A

actions, viewing in History panel, 90

Adobe FrameMaker 9

    keyboard shortcuts for, 137

    structured capabilities, 4

Align panel, opening, 92

anchor symbol

    displaying in tables, 134

    identifying, 100

Anchored Frame

    icon, 103

    panel, 109

anchored frames

    copying, 107

    importing graphics into, 98–100

    moving graphics in, 103

    placing graphics in, 108

    positioning outside columns, 104–106

    resizing, 100–103

    selected status of, 100

Anchoring Position property, setting, 109

asterisk (*), appearance in status bar, 50

autonumbers

    adding colors to, 69–72

    applying character format for, 71–72

    using with chapter titles, 41–42

    using with numbered lists, 37–38

B

\b (bullet), inserting in bulleted list, 40

body cells, formatting in tables, 155

body pages

    creating framesecond text frame for, 57–61

    displaying, 49, 51

body rows, using in tables, 132

body text

    formatting, 33–35

    frame, using, 48

bolded text, adding colors to, 69–70

book chapters

    looking at, 194–195

    page numbering, 199–200

Book Error log, producing, 252

book file

    contents of, 220

    creating, 191–193

    explained, 188

    main file menu for, 192

Book panel, opening, 188

book window

    appearance of, 192

    opening files from, 194–195

    rearranging files in, 194

    using context menus in, 201

headlines, separating from text, 26–27

high.bold character format, using, 69

History panel, viewing last actions with, 90

horizontal line, drawing, 90

horizontal movement, constraining, 79

HTML (Hypertext Markup Language), saving as, 258–259

hypertext cross-reference, formatting, 255–257. *See also* cross-references

hypertext links. *See also* links
 including in index entries, 220
 testing, 254
 using with index, 252–253
 using with TOC, 252–253

I

icons versus panels, 11

Import option, using with tables, 149

Imported Graphic Scaling dialog box, 82, 99

imported table data, formatting, 149–152. *See also* tables

Inconsistent Numbering, displaying for TOC, 212

indents
 applying to numbered lists, 36
 applying to paragraphs, 34–35
 changing, 33
 measurement of, 34

index
 adding to book, 220–221
 changing number of columns in, 222
 changing page layout, 222–223
 displaying pagination properties for, 224
 formatting group titles, 228–229
 formatting main entries, 224–225
 formatting subentries, 225–227
 generating, 221
 including links in, 250–252
 using hypertext with, 252–253

index entries
 adding primary and secondary, 229–230
 editing, 230–231

including hypertext links in, 220

index filename, displaying, 221

inline graphics, using, 108–109

interface preferences, setting for documents, 9

IX suffix, using with indexes, 221

K

keyboard shortcuts
 for AdobeFrameMaker 9, 137
 Anchoring Position property, 109
 cell navigation in tables, 134
 cell selection in tables, 151
 Find command, 211
 inserting row in table, 135
 moving lines point by point, 90
 Open File dialog box, 9
 Paragraph Designer, 53
 redrawing display, 106, 156
 refreshing screen view, 33
 saving files, 25
 updating display, 33

L

Learn feature, using with Spelling Checker, 126

Level1IX main entries, formatting for index, 224

Level2IX subentries, formatting, 225–227

line end, setting in Tools palette, 89

line spacing, changing, 31, 34

lines
 adjusting vertical positions of, 90
 beginning for anchored frame, 98
 copying to Left master page, 93
 drawing, 88–90
 moving point by point, 90
 thickness of, 89

<link.hyper> format, using, 257

links. *See also* hypertext links
 including in index, 250–252
 including in TOC, 250–252